Anthropology is a complex, wide-ranging, and ever changing field. Yet, despite its diversity, certain major themes do occur in the understandings of the world that anthropologists have offered. In this clear, coherent, and well-crafted book, James L. Peacock spells out the central concepts, distinctive methodologies, and philosophical as well as practical issues of cultural anthropology. Designed to supplement standard textbooks and monographs, the book focuses on the premises that underlie the facts that the former kinds of works generally present. Free from unnecessarily abstract theoretical language and based in compelling concrete anecdote and engaging illustration, it is written in terms understandable to the anthropological novice, as well as being of value to the professional.

The book's three main concerns are the substance, method, and significance of anthropology. In his discussion of substance, Peacock examines the major assumptions and conclusions of anthropology, such as the concept of culture, as well as holism. In writing about method, he explores the distinctive character of ethnographic fieldwork and raises questions of interpretation and comparison. Finally, he considers the relevance of anthropology with respect to both its practical application and what it contributes to understanding of human affairs.

Using the photographic metaphors of "harsh light" and "soft focus," Peacock characterizes the anthropological worldview as consisting of two elements: on the one hand, a concern with the basic reality of the human condition, free of cultural influence; on the other, a broadly based holism that attempts to grasp all aspects of that condition, including its relation to the anthropologist. His book will appeal widely to readers interested in anthropology, at all levels.

James L. Peacock has been Professor of Anthropology at the University of North Carolina at Chapel Hill since 1973. His previous publications include *Rites of Modernization*, 1968; *The Human Direction*, 1970; *Indonesia: Anthropological Perspective*, 1973; *Consciousness and Change*, 1975; *Muslim Puritans*, 1978; and *Purifying the Faith*, 1978.

The anthropological lens

The anthropological lens

Harsh light, soft focus

James L. Peacock
University of North Carolina at Chapel Hill

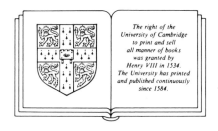

The right of the
University of Cambridge
to print and sell
all manner of books
was granted by
Henry VIII in 1534.
The University has printed
and published continuously
since 1584.

Cambridge University Press

Cambridge
London   New York   New Rochelle
Melbourne   Sydney

Published by the Press Syndicate of the University of Cambridge
The Pitt Building, Trumpington Street, Cambridge CB2 1RP
32 East 57th Street, New York, NY 10022, USA
10 Stamford Road, Oakleigh, Melbourne 3166, Australia

First published 1986

Printed in the United States of America

Library of Congress Cataloging-in-Publication Data
Peacock, James L.
The anthropological lens.
Includes index.
1. Anthropology – Philosophy.   I. Title.
GN33.P358   1986   301'.01   86–13696
ISBN 0 521 33160 9 (hard covers)
ISBN 0 521 33748 8 (paperback)

British Library Cataloging in Publication applied for

25330

Contents

Preface

Can you see the moon? Can you see it seen ...
                    Gertrude Stein, *A Circular Play*

Fall semester began, and I gave the first lecture in an introductory course in anthropology. This course, at a state university, was being taught in the gymnasium and was heavily attended by people whose clothing and demeanor suggested more interest in sports than in study. The class ended, and I asked if there were questions. I was startled when a young man inquired, "What's your hermeneutic?"

"Hermeneutic" in the narrow sense pertains to the study of texts in order to interpret their meaning. This student used the term in a broad sense. He wanted to know the meaning of this course. Perhaps he wanted to know the meaning of anthropology.

The student's question was profound. This book attempts to answer it, at an elementary level. The study of a field like anthropology can be all sound and fury, signifying nothing: exciting facts without sufficient understanding of their meanings. Introductory courses teach such facts. Such courses tell about "bones and stones," as some students term human fossils and artifacts; the varieties of economies, governments, and family organizations throughout the world; how grammars of language vary as we move out of our Indo-European heritage to exotic cultures. What is meant by all this information?

Meaning at a certain level is given by substantive synthesis. All these facts can be made to compose a picture of human existence. The stones and bones can be woven into a story of human origins and evolution. The varieties of social life and languages can display pattern in human culture. Such a panoramic synthesis of human existence is an important objective of anthropology, and a major purpose of introductory courses is to provide such a picture. Knowing these facts and weaving them into a coherent synthesis, one still does not grasp the full meaning of the anthropological perspective. My wife's elderly uncle recently went to a meeting and heard a speech. When he came home, someone asked, "What did the man say?" The old man replied, "He didn't say."

Every statement of fact in anthropology or any other discipline is like the statements of the speaker who said something but did not say what he was saying. The speaker spoke but did not get across what he meant: What was his point? What did he imply? What were the assumptions behind his statements? Only by grasping the assumptions behind statements do we begin to comprehend their meaning. Such understanding is what we seek in exploring the question, What is the anthropological perspective? Through what kind of lens does the anthropologist view the world?

Asking the question, one immediately encounters a problem. Does anthropology have just one lens – a single perspective? There are as many perspectives as there are anthropologists. Consider three autobiographical accounts. Margaret Mead, in her autobiography *Blackberry Winter*, saw anthropology as intimate interpersonal understanding. She extended insights and experiences from her own childhood and family to encompass the entire human family, including the various cultures – in Samoa, in Bali, in New Guinea – where she lived and studied. Anthropologist Richard MacNeish presented a different picture in his autobiographical account *The Science of Archaeology?*. No families – in fact, no living people – appear in the landscapes featured in MacNeish's account. His world is not intimate social circles but the outdoors, broad vistas of adventure and travel from arctic Canada to tropical America, where he searched for potsherds, fossil seeds, and other archaeological remains. Hovering somewhere between the perspectives of Mead and MacNeish is *Tristes Tropiques*, the enchanting autobiographical travelogue by French anthropologist Claude Lévi-Strauss. Lévi-Strauss recounts his experiences with living peoples, but they are hardly portrayed as intimates in a family circle. Instead they are depicted rather objectively and analytically as ciphers, carriers of abstract meanings that are part of some vast system of information that for Lévi-Strauss is the raison d'être of existence. Encountering such varied perspectives, one remembers the doggerel: "Two men look out from the self-same bars; one sees mud, the other sees stars."

To construct a single perspective that encompasses the variety of anthropological viewpoints is impossible, except at a very general level. Yet certain major themes do recur in the understandings set forth by anthropologists. These do compose a broadly held perspective that, if grasped, can helpfully (if not exhaustively) explain some of the meanings and implications of the subject matter. Even so tentative and limited a formulation – and it must be tentative and limited not only because of anthropology's diversity but also because of its incessant change – can be of use.

Objectives

This book is aimed at several types of readers. The neophyte, just beginning the study of anthropology, can profit from understanding something of the philosophy of what he is getting into (and soon, no doubt, will get out of). Middle-level students will profit from examining the premises of the field as they move into specialized topics within it. Advanced students or professionals may find some use in a backward look at that of which they are a part.

This work is not a textbook; it does not catalog the facts of human life as an introductory anthropology textbook does. Instead, it can supplement such a text by elucidating the worldview or perspective that lies behind its subject matter.

Nor is this book an academic treatise, exhaustively surveying the theoretical and methodological writings of the discipline and training the full force of critical analysis on these. Especially, it attempts no full-scale philosophical critique like one a professional philosopher might attempt; instead, it is a somewhat philosophically oriented glance at anthropology by an anthropologist.

Neither textbook nor academic treatise, this book endeavors to combine analysis and anecdote. In place of esoteric fact and academic reference, illustrative material is frequently drawn from common experience. If lighthearted, the work is serious-minded. While avoiding extensive citation of authors and texts, it does endeavor to reflect the deeper issues of the discipline.

A final caution: The work does not give "equal time" to all fields of anthropology. It gives less emphasis to biological, archaeological, and linguistic anthropology than to social and cultural anthropology, though striving to encompass all as parts of a holistic view. Perhaps it is accurate to say that the point of view is that of sociocultural anthropology, or of one sociocultural anthropologist.

Outline and approach

This book is divided into three chapters, on the substance, the method, and the significance of anthropology, respectively.

By substance is meant both the major assumptions and major conclusions of anthropology: its major concepts, illustrated through its findings. Culture – a set of shared understandings – is the dominant concept in anthropology. Yet culture is part of a broad view of human existence that anthropologists term "holistic." Some anthropologists would not so strongly emphasize either culture or holism; nevertheless, taking anthropology as a whole in its full history and breadth, these concepts loom as dominant.

Chapter 2 treats method: the way anthropologists go about learning what they learn. Fieldwork is the distinctive method of anthropology. The peculiarly demanding combination of physical hardship, psychological disorientation, and intellectual challenge that constitutes fieldwork can be understood only by those who have done it. In fact, even for these, memory dims, so that the experience is difficult to recall and describe sharply. In order to draw nearer to a sense of what fieldwork entails, this chapter begins with experiences familiar to most of us, then works toward isolating those features central to the field experience.

Fieldwork is not merely experience. It is also method. Anthropology has distinctive ways of contributing to scientific and humanistic understanding. Questions of interpretation and comparison are considered with respect to this discipline, which seeks both minute detail and broad understanding.

The final chapter attempts to formulate perspectives that unite themes of substance and method. It suggests that no single framework unites the entire discipline but that two major ones compete: one based more on the natural sciences; the other, on the humanities. In conclusion, it explores the relevance and significance of anthropology with respect to both practical application and general understanding in human affairs.

The quotations at the head of each chapter signal a movement from wonder to skepticism to speculation, in accord with the movement of chapters from substance to method to significance. The quotations are biblical, but it is their general connotation of attitude rather than specific theological doctrine that is pertinent here. There is a certain message, however, in the framing of analysis within religious imagery. Analysis is grounded in belief; the premise of rationality – that truth is to be found through logic – is itself not provable through logic but is ultimately a matter of faith.

The quotation from Gertrude Stein that heads the Preface refers to the notion of a perspective. One sees the moon (or anything else); one asks about the moon, the object seen, and one also asks about the *seeing* – *how* one sees or how *one* sees. These latter questions are about perspective. "Lens" in the book's title is analogous to "perspective"; both determine – the one optically, the other mentally – what one sees.

A guiding image: harsh light and soft focus
In the physics of photography, the brighter the light, the smaller the aperture of the lens; with more light, a smaller hole is sufficient to transmit the image to the film. And the smaller the aperture, the larger is the depth of field. That is, the photographer can include in focus the background and foreground of the object as well as the object itself. If this field could be extended infinitely, it could include even the camera.

Anthropology is not imprisoned in the laws of optics, nor is it exclusively visual; but a visual analogy may help us think concretely. Imagine a photographer who favors bright, harsh light – conditions where glare is intense. Imagine also that he seeks depth of field – to include in focus the foreground and background as well as the object itself. Anthropology seeks conditions of harsh light; this may be literally true, inasmuch as anthropologists tend to work in settings exposed to the intense sun of desert and tropics, but it is also true metaphorically in that anthropologists usually seek to do their work in conditions that are in some sense harsh, so as to expose the raw and elemental, the fundamentals of human nature stripped of the fluff of civilization. Within those settings, anthropology focuses softly rather than sharply: Rather than focus narrowly on the object, anthropology blurs the boundary between object and milieu so as to include not only the object but also its background, side-ground, and foreground; this perception of the total milieu we call holism. Were this holistic field of vision extended far enough, it would include the perceiver as well as the object perceived, and this too is a concern of anthropology, which recognizes the subjective as well as the objective aspect of knowledge.

Apologies and acknowledgments

With apologies, I adhere to the convention of using the pronoun "he" rather than "he/she," "she/he" "s/he," or "she" to refer to third persons whose gender is not specified. The practice is editorial, not ideological.

I thank Stanford University Press for permission to quote from Gregory Bateson, *Naven* (1958 ed.), p. 262; Curtis Brown Ltd. for permission to quote from Lincoln Barnett, *The Universe and Dr. Einstein* (1948 ed.), pp. 8 and 9; Oxford University Press for permission to quote from E. E. Evans-Pritchard, *The Nuer* (1940 ed.), pp. 12–13; Pantheon Books, Random House for permission to quote from Boris Pasternak, *Dr. Zhivago*, trans. Max Hayward and Manya Harari (1958 ed.), pp. 270–1; the University of California Press for permission to quote from Rodney Needham, *Against the Tranquility of Axioms* (1983 ed.), p. 33; and the Musée d'Orsay, Paris, for permission to reproduce Henri Rousseau, *La Charmeuse de Serpents*.

Special gratitude is due to the John Simon Guggenheim Foundation and to the University of North Carolina at Chapel Hill, which supported a year at Oxford University when this project was begun; to Rodney Needham, All Souls College, and the Institute of Social Anthropology, gracious hosts at Oxford; to family, students, and friends for indispensable assistance and suggestions: John Baggett, Keith Basso, Carolyn Bloomer, David Brown, Richard Eckley, Louly Fowler, Marilyn Grunkemeyer, Steven Klein, Christine Loken-Kim, Edwin Lonergan, Karen McIntyre, Stuart Marks, and Louly Peacock. My father and mother I thank for many things.

1

Substance

Behold! I tell you a mystery!
1 Corinthians 15:51–2

What is life? What is the essence of human existence? Of what does experience consist?

Anthropology offers a variety of answers to these questions. This variety can be reduced to several major themes. Most prominent, perhaps, is this: Human life should be viewed as a whole – a configuration interwoven of many forces and aspects, all organized by culture.

It's real!: culture beheld

Surabaya – hot, crowded, impoverished – is a port city of Java, which is the most populous island of the world's fifth largest nation, Indonesia. In 1962, when I was doing fieldwork in Surabaya, an estimated 75,000 of its million inhabitants were beggars. Most people were undernourished, living on a third the food Westerners eat. Inflation had run away; prices were tripling monthly, and monthly wages were enough for only a few days of each month. The family with whom my wife and I were living, in a shantytown near the railroad tracks, were surviving but barely. Medicine was difficult to obtain; communications were uncertain; transportation, an adventure. The city was dominated by the Communist party, which at the time was the second largest in Asia and was poised for revolution. Instability, hardship, and anxiety characterized this period titled by a recent film "The Year of Living Dangerously."

Amazingly, despite the hard and uncertain conditions of life, the exquisitely refined values of Javanese culture were sustained. If one visited a house, one would be seated at a small table and served a drink of tea or sweetened water. One could not straightaway drink but had to wait until host or hostess gave the command, a crooned word, "Manggoooooooo," after which both of you would drink. Thus began the formalized ceremony of a Javanese visit, properly terminated by intoning in the same refined language, "Now I ask permission to leave." Such ceremonialism was so solidly entrenched and well understood in Javanese life that it was even the subject of working-class theater: A clown, playing the host, would substitute for the high Javanese invitation "Drink" the crude Javanese command "Slurp it up," alluding to the animal impulse beneath the polite facade. But the civilized veneer, if satirized, was deeply valued.

The conventions of refined language and manners were elaborated also in a vast complex of ceremonial life. A Javanese wedding of an ordinary couple would not suffer in pomp and pageantry by comparison to the Royal Wedding. Exquisitely graceful dances, inspired by the Javanese courts, were performed not only in the courts on auspicious occasions but on ordinary days by slum children on rickety bamboo stages. Cults in mysticism and meditation abounded, and ordinary people worrying about their next meal would expound esoteric philosophies and theorize about the profundities of Javanese civilization.

All of this was Javanese culture. The manners, ceremonies, language, arts, and philosophies were so deeply ingrained that they did not disappear under awful conditions. The culture is as much a way of life as the deformed beggars, haggling merchants, and corrupt politicians; it still flourishes, even after a time of violence when, following "the year of living dangerously," an estimated half-million Indonesians were massacred and turbulent changes occurred.

As in this example, most anthropological fieldwork has been done in settings harsh, remote, or both – rarely in the comfortable suburbs or salons that we associate with culture and civilization. Yet out of these exposures to "harsh light" has come an appreciation of what we have termed culture – an enduring way of thinking and of ordering our lives that survives the struggle to survive. Whatever culture is, "it's real." At least something is, which we can conveniently label "culture."

Culture defined
In surveying the anthropological definitions of culture, one is reminded of Elizabeth Barrett Browning's lines: "How do I love thee? Let me count the ways..." Anthropologists have promiscuously showered affection on the notion of culture, a notion so obvious in their experience and so central to their discipline. Yet they have never agreed on a single definition. Certain commonalities are, however, apparent.

The classic definition was provided by Sir Edward Tylor, the founder of social anthropology, in 1871: "Culture... taken in its wide ethnographic sense is that complex whole which includes knowledge, belief, art, morals, law, custom, and any other capabilities and habits acquired by man as a member of society."[1]

In Tylor's definition, culture is "acquired by man as a member of society." This implies that culture is learned, rather than inherited biologically. It implies further that culture is social; it is shared, rather than a property of the individual. On these two features of culture, most anthropologists would agree. Some would distinguish the society of ants or bees from that of humans in that ant or bee society, although boasting division of labor (as between queens and workers) and other traits akin to human social organization, is seemingly an expression of inherited or instinctual rather than learned patterns. Others might distinguish the mental productions of the psychotic from that of a culture; the psychotic's delusion is peculiar to himself, whereas the ideas in a culture, though sometimes equally bizarre, are shared rather than borne alone.

These features — that culture is learned and shared — state conditions of culture. But what is culture itself? Tylor lists several elements of culture: "knowledge, belief, art, morals, law, custom, and any other capabilities and habits acquired by man as a member of society." This list is long. It seems to include just about anything one can learn and share. Anthropologists have narrowed the list in different ways. Some have emphasized the mental or attitudinal rather than the behavioral aspect of culture. In this view, culture is not behavior itself but the shared understandings that guide behavior and are expressed in behavior. How do we learn about these understandings? Through observing behaviors and other visible or audible forms that manifest them. Difficulties in this formulation need not detain us now. Our present task is to grasp that something – some kind of pattern or organized disposition – is expressed in behaviors characteristic of each group of people. We need to sense the importance of these patterns and the power they have in organizing our lives.

The example from Surabaya is extreme; here people are maintaining culture under conditions imposing great strain. One thinks of other examples in history. Jan Bokelson's utopian religious community at Münster was besieged in 1535 by the royal armies of the Rhine. Cut off from food, the faithful were forced to celebrate the glories of God by performing athletic feats while starving to death. Most anthropological studies have not been carried out under conditions so severe as this, but, as noted, most have been carried out under conditions that were in some way harsh. Yet these are the experiences that have fueled the anthropological conviction that human culture has force and power: If culture survives here, it will prevail anywhere.

What are some of the qualities of culture that render it powerful?

Culture is taken for granted. In the metaphor of Edward Hall, culture is a "silent language."[2] Traditions and conventions are silent in the sense that they are often unconscious. People who claim to act rationally, to be motivated only by considerations such as efficiency, unconsciously are guided by rigid and pervasive traditions. To lay bare these traditions is a central task of the anthropologist, not to mention the satirist. Hall's work exemplifies this approach.

Hall points out that for centuries the West has conceived of time as linear. Time is a line stretching between the past and the future, divided into centuries, years, months, weeks, days, hours, minutes, and seconds. Every event we unhesitatingly classify along that line: The Age of Dinosaurs is many intervals back, World War II is near our present position; gestation may stretch nine months along the line, the act of birth is only a point. The future is similarly envisioned as a movement along a line: Nations follow five-year plans and try to progress; individuals have careers. Everyone should make a determined movement down the line and overcome obstacles and interruptions in order to "get ahead." This way of thinking is embedded in our culture from many sources. It is in our language, which, unlike many non-European languages, has tense; it categorizes experience in past, present, and future. It is in our Judeo-Christian religious tradition, which imagines that we have a history – a past progressing from the creation of the world through Abraham, Moses, and the prophets – and a future. It has been intensified by the machine age, which forces us to mechanize, plan, sequentialize with precision. We have been taught this way of thinking in schools, which carry us through a sequence of grades toward graduation; by our proverbs, which tell us that time is money, that time waits for no man, that time should be saved and not wasted. We have grown up thinking about time in this linear way. We think this way without thinking about the way we are thinking. We take this way of thinking for granted.

Anthropologists like Hall teach us that not everybody thinks this way. The Trobriand Islanders of the Western Pacific reportedly held different assumptions. It is said that, unlike the hard-driving achiever, the Trobrianders did not particularly mind interruptions or even see an obstacle to their completing a task as an interruption. To them, time was not so much a line along which one moved as it was a puddle in which one sat, splashed, or wallowed. Trobrianders imagined time as a directionless configuration rather than a directional line.

One should, of course, hasten to caution against the danger of stereotyping a culture. In Java, I once was introduced as a speaker on a program by the phrase, "Now Mr. James will *mengisi waktu*," which means "fill up time." I was inclined to interpret this as part of the elaborate ceremonialism noted earlier: that people cared less about what I said or accomplished than that I filled a slot in the ceremony. This sort of nonlinear pattern can be seen in Javanese life, where time is traditionally based on cycles rather than progressions and is associated with Hindu-Buddhist traditions; but Western linear calendars and drives toward striving and achieving are apparent too.

That sense of time varies is obvious to anyone who looks and listens, for differences are apparent even within our own society. Black time occasionally differs from white time, and other ethnic and regional variations are noticeable too: "I'd love you in a New York minute but take my Texas time," goes a country and western song. Despite noticing the variations, most of us take for granted whatever notion of time is governing us. Achievers who claim simply to act efficiently and rationally are really performing a giant ritual expressing traditions of their particular culture and subculture. One may choose consciously a particular career or life-style and may justify a particular creed or set of values and goals, but no one ever uncovers all of the taken-for-granted premises that are part of one's culture – the "tacit knowledge" by which one lives in the world.

Culture is shared. Linguistic anthropology offers one of the most striking examples of this: the phoneme. The phoneme is a feature of sound that is crucial for communication. If you compare the way different people talk, even those who speak the same language and have the same "accent," you can hear all kinds of variations. Speakers use different pitch, volume, tone quality, stress, and patterns of breathing. They have different kinds of vocal organs, and some may even lack teeth or have other peculiarities. Incredibly, despite these differences, they communicate. How does language accomplish this? Every language identifies a small number of distinctions in sound (some languages have as few as a dozen, none have more than ninety, English has about forty) that are absolutely critical; these distinctions are phonemes. So long as these are produced and understood, communication can occur. For example, in English it is necessary that the speaker distinguish between "b" and "p" (otherwise he would confuse "pin" and "bin," "bull" and "pull," "pan" and "ban"). It is not necessary that he make all possible distinctions. Some that are critical in other languages make no difference in ours. For example, such Asian languages as Chinese and Thai distinguish tones that change the meanings of words. Without practice, an English-speaker cannot even hear the difference between such tones, much less reproduce them, for tonal difference is not phonemic in English.

Shared patterning in language illustrates a feature of culture that has impressed anthropologists and anyone else who has thought about it. With no individual intending or planning it, a group establishes rules, codes, values, and conventions that its members share. Not confined to any single person, shared culture is beyond the control of any single person; it takes on a power of its own.

Encounter with the other
Once in a small-town mosque in Java, a congregation of several hundred prayed that I convert to Islam. What was the source of

my resistance? For one thing, I had taken the stance of the "researcher," the fieldworker "studying" this tradition, rather than the stance of a believer in one thing open to something else. In fact, when the Muslim group once asked me, "What is your religion?" I replied, "My religion is anthropology"; I meant that I was a student of belief, rather than a believer. At a deeper level, to convert would have meant giving up a cultural identity as well as accepting a religious commitment.

Encounter with the other intensifies awareness of one's own cultural identity. This principle explains the anthropologist's insistence on fieldwork in some alien setting, and it explains his use of comparison between the foreign and the familiar. The fish is the last to understand the water; perhaps he can do so in contrast to the land. Some kind of encounter with the other is necessary to grasp the power and reality of culture.

Culture, then, is a name anthropologists give to the taken-for-granted but powerfully influential understandings and codes that are learned and shared by members of a group. Different schools and branches of anthropology differ in the emphasis they give to culture (for example, British social anthropology emphasizes more the social context of culture, whereas American cultural anthropology emphasizes culture itself), but the concept of culture is important throughout anthropology. A major mission and contribution of anthropology has long been, and continues to be, to enhance our awareness of the power and reality of culture in our existence.

Anthropology defined: a holistic discipline

"As few as you can, as many as you must" was John Stuart Mill's advice concerning definitions. His British countrymen excelled in definitions at once terse and acerbic. Oats are what Englishmen feed to horses and Scotsmen to men, according to Samuel Johnson, and Oscar Wilde termed the fox hunter "the unspeakable in pursuit of the inedible." Perhaps the wittiest definition of anthropology is Margaret Mead's "the study of man, embracing women." In a way, the purpose of this entire volume is to define anthropology, so we begin by providing some idea of what anthropology is about before we proceed.

Anthropology is what anthropologists do. That is a succinct way

to characterize the discipline, and an approach some favor. But is
it correct? Obviously it is wrong. Anthropologists spend much of
their time doing what everybody else does. They sleep and eat,
work (sporadically), talk (interminably), travel (frequently). These
doings are not all anthropology. What about the things anthropologists do that only they, and no others, do? Now we approach
precision, but the definition is still inadequate. Owing to the demands of their research, anthropologists may spend more time than
most people traveling to exotic places and recovering from exotic
diseases; these traits are distinctive, but do travel and disease define
anthropology? What we need to know is what anthropologists do
as anthropologists – the part of their activity that constitutes anthropology. But how is one to know when anthropologists act as
anthropologists without first knowing what anthropology is? We
are back where we started.

One might begin with activities but now select those generally
regarded as "professional." Such a list would include all of the
different kinds of research that anthropologists do, from digging
up fossils to living among the people in contemporary out-of-the-
way places. Some notion of the range of subject matter treated by
anthropology is given by a list of such courses taught in college.
The following list is from a term's offerings in a middle-sized department in an American state university:

Human Evolution and Adaptation
Old World Prehistory
Principles of Archaeology
Culture Change and Underdeveloped Areas
Culture and Personality
Magic, Ritual, and Belief
Aboriginal Cultures of Mexico and Central America
Indians of North America
Art and Culture
Contemporary Japanese Society
Urban Anthropology
Emergence of the State
Anthropology and Education
Observation and Interpretation of Religious Action
Cross-Cultural Research

Human Osteology
Seminar in Transcultural Psychiatry
Seminar in Phenomenological Anthropology
Seminar in Ethnobotany
Field Research

For comparison, consider this list of courses offered in a term at a British university (Oxford):

ETHNOLOGY
Technology of Simple Societies
Social Ecological Systems
Social Ecology (lectures)
Social Ecology (classes)

PREHISTORY ARCHAEOLOGY
The Palaeolithic Period
Practical Class
Iron Age Communities in Europe
Science and Archaeology
Aspects of African Archaeology

HUMAN BIOLOGY
Practical Class: Stress Physiology
Human Genetics and Medicine
Introductory Population Genetics
Biochemical Variation in Man
Practical Class
Human Variation
Interactive Computing by BASIC (1)
Interactive Computing by BASIC (2)

SOCIAL ANTHROPOLOGY
Analyses
Research Class
Mind, Body, and Spirit Among the Uduk
Further Anthropological Analyses
Social Anthropology and Identity: Some Celtic Cases
Peoples of the Nile Basin (class)
The Historical Aspects of Anthropology (Diploma Class for
    students in Social Anthropology)

Peoples of Latin America
Settled Arab Communities

The variety and range of topics in anthropology are vast. They include the full length of human history and prehistory, spanning millions of years. They encompass the globe, excluding no space or group. In terms of aspects, anthropology includes the biological as well as the cultural, the economic and psychological, the aesthetic and political. Methods range from quantitative to qualitative, from archaeological to sociological, and from particularistic fieldwork to global generalization and philosophizing. So-called relevant and topical issues include feminism, racism, population explosions, crises of meaning and disbelief, evolutionism and creationism. Anthropology encroaches on the territory of the sciences as well as the humanities, and transcends the conventional boundaries of both while addressing questions to the distant past and the pressing present – perhaps with implications for the future.

This broad view, sometimes termed "holistic," is perhaps the most striking single quality of anthropology. Whatever definition of anthropology one chooses, it should stress that this is a discipline for understanding humankind in its many facets – holistically.

If anthropology tries to see everything and everywhere, then does it have a distinctive focus? As was suggested earlier, that focus is culture. This is not to say that anthropology is exclusively preoccupied with culture; it is very much concerned with what some might term the "harsh reality" of the material world as well. But anthropological studies are distinctive in attempting to connect this material world to cultural meanings. Studies of fossil humans and other skeletal remains uncovered by archaeologists and physical anthropologists may result in analysis of the anatomy of skulls and teeth and the geology of habitat, but ultimately such studies, if they are anthropological, relate such features to human creations: tools, paintings, speech. Linguistic studies of language may plot the physics of sound – its frequency, volume, and overtones – but ultimately, in anthropological linguistics, such analysis is "phonemic"; that is, physical sounds are understood as categories experienced and constructed by humans as part of their culture. Economic anthropologists may measure the value of material goods exchanged, but these exchanges are seen as grounded in rules and meanings shared by their participants. The emphasis within anthropology is clear when we compare neighboring fields outside. The physical anthropologist resembles the biologist; the archaeologist, the geologist; the economic anthropologist, the economist; but, generally speaking, each anthropologist differs from his counterpart in giving greater emphasis to culture – though always within a holistic framework.

Perceiving holistically

A Russian factory worker, it is told, was in the habit of pushing the wheelbarrow through the factory gate at quitting time. Every evening the guards would inspect the wheelbarrow and, finding it empty, let the worker pass. After some months, it was discovered that the worker was stealing wheelbarrows.

The guards' fallacy was to inspect the contents and not the container, to focus, too narrowly, on the parts and not the whole. Empathizing with the guards, we are reminded of how we often fail to see holistically – how we are blinded by our own perspective. This lesson can be applied to familiar experiences.

Who am I? This is a question well known in our culture. Most of us reared in the West at least think there *is* an "I." I exist, as a distinct individual, a personality separated by my skin from the outside. Spit on your hand. Swallow that spittle. Most would prefer not to do so. Inside me, that spittle is simply saliva and I give it little thought, but once it is outside myself it is not myself anymore. I wipe it off my hand.

This little experiment illustrates how each of us distinguishes self from other. Self is a discrete, bounded entity. This way of thinking may be familiar, but it is not necessarily the only way to think about the self. It is the way our culture teaches us. Let us remind ourselves of some of the sources of this culture. Consider, for example, a book that has been extremely influential in Anglo-American philosophy, the masterwork of the seventeenth-century British philosopher Thomas Hobbes: *Leviathan*.[3]

Hobbes begins with the individual. For him, the individual is the elementary unit of human experience. The individual is also the building block of society and of all else. This is the assumption of individualism, the doctrine that the individual is the basic reality whereas society is a construct. One may think, "How could it be otherwise?" Yet other philosophies start with other assumptions.

According to Hobbes, individuals have passions. They sense and reason, but they also will and want. They want status, property, and the like. In Hobbes's view, this is human nature, the character of man in his natural state.

Unfortunately, property and power are scarce. Want causes competition and conflict. Humans left to their own inclinations soon degenerate into a war of "everyman against everyman." (This view of human nature, incidentally, continues to be expressed in British literature, still reflecting the Hobbesian philosophy. In *Lord of the Flies*, by William Golding, boys left on a tropical island rapidly degenerate into fighting hordes without justice or compassion. The Orcs in Tolkien's *Lord of the Rings* personify this human tendency exaggerated into a disgusting tribe of monsters. And, of course, this Hobbesian view of human nature lies behind the so-called law-and-order advocates in American society.)

Hobbes warned that if men are left in their natural state, they will be at each other's throats, and life will be, in his famous phrase, "Nasty, brutish, and short."

Humans must counter their nasty natures by introducing societal controls. They have therefore traded freedom for order, which is necessary for survival. They accept the rule of someone, in order to protect themselves against everyone. Thus is created government, the Leviathan.

But this Leviathan is a monster, an artificial creation. In a picture appearing in the original edition of Hobbes's work, Leviathan is a huge man, composed of many small men, bearing the face of none other than the sardonic philosopher Hobbes himself.

A powerful and compelling vision! (It is, of course, more powerful and compelling to read in the original than in summary.) Hobbes exemplifies the philosophy of individualism.

Hobbes is not, of course, the sole source of individualism, merely a notably lucid and forceful representative. Many influences converge to teach us individualism. Western languages, for example, emphasize the personal pronoun "I" – an emphasis not always present in other languages. Protestant Christian tradition emphasizes that it is the individual self, as an independent unit, which is damned to eternal suffering in hell or saved for eternal bliss in heaven. Other emphases are present in other religions; for example, in early Judaism it was the nation that God punished or rewarded. One person, one vote is the rule in American democracy, but not, say, in early-twentieth-century Japan, where it was the household head who voted, representing the household group. Each of us is given a distinct name, which we identify with ourselves so much that one feels a bit odd to meet someone else with the same name; in some cultures, however, a person is known not by a name peculiar to himself but by a name that links him to someone else, as in the custom of calling parents by the names of their children: "parent of X." Each of us has a distinct social security or identity number, each of us is assigned a separate seat on an airplane, each of us is said to have a unique set of fingerprints. In a thousand ways, our culture emphasizes the uniqueness and discrete identity of the individual.

Individualism sees the whole made from the parts. One starts with the parts, namely individuals, and builds wholes, namely societies. The parts, the individuals, are the basic, real, and natural reality. One can, as Hobbes suggested, construct a commonwealth, but this whole is artificial and fragile.

Emile Durkheim, the French philosopher and sociologist who was the inspiration of much anthropological study of society, took the opposite viewpoint. Durkheim took as basic reality not the individual but the society. He began with the whole, not the parts. Durkheim argued that unless society had come to exist, the individual – as a sensing, reasoning creature, a human – could never have come to exist. He also argued that in our ongoing existence, the group is more fundamental than the individual.[4]

Durkheim's argument is based in part on parallels between human thought and the patterning of society. For example, thought proceeds by classification, by division into classes. Society is constructed similarly.[5] From such parallels, Durkheim argues that society is the basis for thought.

Durkheim's viewpoint resonates with the anthropological experience and perspective. Anthropologists have done much of their research in societies that are more collectivistic than our own. Classically, anthropologists studied so-called primitives: societies based on hunting and gathering or horticulture, organized around bonds of kinship, and sustaining a collective life grounded in oral tradition and ritual.[6] Such societies now survive only in remote jungles, mountains, and islands, constituting about six percent of the world's population today; but only some ten thousand years ago, all people were of this type. Their kind of existence is much more basic in human history than our kind.

In such societies, the group – the community and clan – has power difficult for us to imagine. The dramatic instances are easiest to cite. In "voodoo death," for example, if the group declares a person dead, he dies.[7] Conversely, in rituals of healing, if the group declares a person well, he gets well.[8] Here individual consciousness is so deeply enmeshed with group consciousness that it is not accurate to speak of individualism as we know it. (It is also inaccurate to exaggerate the collectivist character of such societies, for they have their individualistic aspects too; yet, in broad comparison with our own lives, the point holds.)

Anthropology, with its perspective spanning the millions of years between human prehistory and the present, acknowledges the pervasiveness of collectivism. From the time of human origins to the first states in the Near East and Asia some ten thousand years ago, humans lived in small bands. Even after the first states were organized, most of life was lived collectively, with government, community, and kinship having priority over the individual. The concept of the individual as we know it really came to exist only a few hundred years ago, as a product of the Reformation, Renaissance, and industrial revolution, and even then it was confined to Western Europe and its colonies. Collectivism has a larger place in human history than individualism.

Reflecting logically rather than historically, one arrives at a similar conclusion. Thought occurs through language, and language is a property of groups; thus thought itself – in the highly symbolic forms developed by humans – is a property of the group.

Finally, the notion of individualism is itself a product of the group. The philosophy of individualism is, after all, a product of Western society. What we term "individual" is a cultural construct.

Instead of Descartes's "I think, therefore I am," the Durkheimian collectivist would assert, "I am, I exist, as part and product of my society and culture, therefore I think."

In short, by taking a Durkheimian point of view, we conclude that our immediate reality – a sense of self – is part of a broad

reality, the society and culture. To say this is simple; to realize it
is more difficult, for we are taught to think individualistically!

A holistic view of nature
The notion of individualism ramifies beyond our perception of our
relation to society. We have come to think of ourselves as separate
from nature. Some of us may admire and enjoy nature – until we
are trapped in a tornado or hurricane, or bitten by a snake or spider
– but the general tenor of modern Western culture has been to set
the individual against nature. One must struggle against nature,
which is a dangerous enemy – in Tennyson's phrase, "red in tooth
and claw." Rooted in Christian theologies that viewed nature as
fallen and evil, and perpetuated by Victorian visions of progress,
modern culture encourages us to conquer, harness, and even destroy
nature. Gregory Bateson, a British anthropologist and biologist,
objects to this view of nature opposing the human individual. In
his *Steps to an Ecology of Mind* [9] and his *Mind and Nature: A
Necessary Unity*,[10] Bateson argues that it is fallacious to imagine
the individual separate from and opposed to the environment. He
argues further that this fallacy is destroying both us and our environment because logically the organism that destroys its environment destroys itself. The unit of survival is not the organism; it is
organism plus environment.

Bateson urges us to realize that the individual and nature are part
of a single whole. A man, an ax, and a tree are part of a system
such that it is arbitrary to draw a line where the man stops and the
ax begins, or the ax stops and the tree begins. If the man cuts down
the tree, it is not just the tree that is affected but the man as well.[11]

This point of view is not peculiar to anthropology but is part of
the approach known as "ecology," which emphasizes the ramified
connections among all living systems. Within ecological studies anthropology is distinctive in recognizing the place of culture. Anthropology has noted, especially, cultural perspectives that emphasize the intimacy between the human and the natural. The Nuer
of Africa, for example, are said to think of their social relationships
in terms of their cattle to such an extent that they do not imagine
the one except in terms of the other; Evans-Pritchard states that "a
Nuer genealogy may sound like an inventory of a kraal [stall].
... Their social idiom is a bovine idiom."[12] The classic pattern of

nature/human unity is known as "totemism." In totemic societies, each group identifies with a natural category: bear, lion, wolf clans, for example. We have pale remnants of this in some spheres, such as sports team names – the Wolfpack, the Yellow Jackets, the Tigers, and the Terrapins. A family that, like mine, bears the name of an animal, may display images of that creature as a kind of totem. And in the work of a sensitive writer such as William Faulkner, one sees a surviving sense of totemism; read "The Bear," or *As I Lay Dying*, where people identify with bears, horses, and even fish. But in true totemic cultures, a person deeply and categorically identifies with his totem. The Bororo of Brazil are said to believe, in certain special ways and contexts, that they are the animal that is their totem.

Recognizing that human groups do experience a certain unity of self and nature, many anthropologists are sympathetic to Bateson's argument. It fits the holistic emphasis in reminding us that just as individual apart from society is an abstraction from the unity of experience, so is "individual" apart from nature.

At another level, one may speak of the relation between man and nature – man's own nature. Hobbes saw this relation, too, as a battle. Reason fights passion; order is achieved by controlling our baser nature. This view has dominated Western psychology, though how control is to be achieved varies with the school of thought.

Freudian psychology seeks control of the passions, the id, the libido, by coming to know them. One renders the unconscious conscious, through psychoanalysis.

British psychology, more directly akin to Hobbes, apparently prefers not to know the baser self. "Morbid introspection" was the British Victorian psychologists' view of exploring inner motives.[13] Just stiffen the upper lip and carry on! The telephone directory of Oxford, England, lists only a fraction of the number of psychiatrists and psychologists listed in the American university town where I live, even though Oxford is much larger. This difference doubtless reflects the psychologizing of America, but Anglo-American culture shares the emphasis on controlling passions. There are numerous American psychologies of control: from Dale Carnegie to behavior modification.

Here we are tracing a particular recent view of self in relation to our baser natures, the passions. This is a Western view, but one also finds parallels in Eastern religious movements, roughly contemporaneous with the origin of Christianity, notably Islam and Buddhism. Chinese examples are noted in recent studies by Joseph Needham.[14] Islam sees passions (*nafsu*) controlled by reason (*akal*) and ethics (*achlak*).[15] Javanese mystical cults that unite Muslim and Buddhist influences depict the passions as colors (such as red) that threaten to explode unless dampened by other colors (such as black and white) – a kind of control brought about by meditation.

Going beyond these historic traditions and considering the gamut of human experience, we discover that the holistic view occurs frequently. In this view, nature, whether our own or external nature, is simply part of the totality of existence. Disease, healing, fears, and hopes, the unconscious and consciousness, are experienced in unity with all life. This deep-rooted sense of unity generates the powerful healing rituals found in tribal contexts from Africa to Malaya to native America. We are rediscovering such unity, to a limited extent, in so-called holistic medicine; much anthropological lore supports the wisdom of these trends, to a point, although they are still imprisoned in our cultural setting.

To think holistically is to see parts as wholes, to try to grasp the broader contexts and frameworks within which people behave and experience. One such framework is culture. Anthropology is concerned not only with holistically analyzing the place of humans in society and in nature but also, and especially, with the way humans construct cultural frameworks in order to render their lives meaningful.

If the Frenchman Emile Durkheim is our seminal philosopher of society, the German Max Weber is our most influential sociologist of meaning. Weber illustrated the process of bestowing meaning through his study of the "Protestant ethic."[16] According to Weber, Calvinist Puritans craved salvation and feared damnation to such an extent that they sought a way to assure themselves that they were saved, not damned. They finally decided that if you "worked like the devil," you could claim to be elected to salvation, for such work gave the appearance of serving God. In this way, Calvinist religion rendered work meaningful – in fact, sacred. As a byproduct, heirs of the Protestant tradition – which is to say, many members of contemporary Western and Westernized cultures – feel guilty if they don't work.

Weber exemplifies a holistic analysis of one stream in Western history. He shows how an activity that we narrowly identify as economic – work, especially in capitalistic business – is in fact only a part of a complex whole that includes a Protestant ethic. Once again, activity that seems merely practical turns out to have deep cultural groundings.

For the anthropologist, this kind of interrelatedness of meaning and life, culture and existence, is best seen in the lives of "primitives," for they attain a greater unity than we. When the Australian Aborigine locates himself within his cosmos, which embraces his natural desert environment, his animal and plant companions, his ancestral spirits, his rites, and his shrines, he is living meaning. He does not merely speculate about God or angel, creation or afterlife. In one ritual, he falls into trance and dreams; and in that dreaming, he identifies with spirits that one may call, after Joseph Conrad, "secret sharers." These secret sharers are his ancestors, but still alive. Thus the Aborigine comes to live, he feels, in the past as well as the future – in the eternal, the "everywhen."[17]

This sort of experience is what anthropologist Rodney Needham implies when he demonstrates that "belief " is not a suitable term for describing much of religious experience.[18] Belief, in fact, best suits those peculiarly textual and theological traditions of Near Eastern origin – Judaism, Islam, and Christianity. A belief is a proposition: I believe there is a God; I believe there is a heaven. The relation of humans to the spiritual is deeper and more complex than this. In my own fieldwork I once asked an Indonesian, "Do you believe [*pertjaja*] in spirits?" He replied, puzzled, "Are you asking, do I believe what spirits tell me when they talk to me?" For him, spirits were not a belief but an unquestionable relationship, part of the unity of his life.

Here, then, are some ways of thinking holistically. One can try to grasp the larger configuration of society, nature, and meaning in which that element which we call "the individual" has a place; one tries to comprehend wholes.

Anthropology encourages this kind of holism at several levels. The first is interpretive, as we have just exemplified. One tries to perceive and understand each experience holistically.

The second level is a way of doing the first. It is the most distinctive kind of anthropological research. It is termed "ethnography," which means a description of a certain way of life, and it is based on "fieldwork" – living with and observing a living group. In fieldwork, the anthropologist traditionally attempts to treat the group's life as a whole – not to isolate some artificially abstracted aspect, such as economics, politics, or nutrition, but to consider all of these as they relate to each other and to other aspects: religion, education, family life, biological, medical, or environmental conditions, art, and so on. In fact, it is both a premise and a conclusion of ethnographic research that existence – especially in a small community – is a web the threads of which cannot be disentangled. To divide this whole into compartments such as economics and politics may be useful for analysis, but one must always remember that the compartments are analytical creations and that the whole must be grasped in order to understand any part.

The third way that anthropology is holistic is in its organization as a discipline. Anthropology unites in one field of study many specialties that treat various aspects of human life: biological, geological, and physical sciences; linguistic, humanistic, social and cultural studies; and archaeological and historical as well as contemporary focuses. If each specialty is analogous to a musical instrument, then anthropology is like a symphony orchestra.

Less elegantly, the individual anthropologist could be compared to the one-man band, which is the fourth mode of holistic integration: within the activities of a single anthropologist. This kind of holism is exemplified by one of the founding fathers of anthropology, Alfred Kroeber. During his long life (1876–1960), Kroeber contributed significantly in archaeology, linguistics, sociocultural anthropology, and related fields in the humanities and natural sciences. He was also, for a time, a practicing psychoanalyst; he founded a museum, excavated in Peru, did extensive fieldwork among Indians of the West Coast and in California, wrote both technical articles and world histories, and was a teacher and administrator. Although the holism exemplified by Kroeber is not common among anthropologists today, the discipline continues to affirm the ideal of integrating some kind of large vision.

Wholes differentiated into parts; analytical constructs
Holism is an important but impossible ideal. You cannot see everywhere or think everything. You must select and emphasize. To do

this, you must categorize and make distinctions. Only in this way can you analyze and understand.

In the physical world, it is relatively easy to do this. Here is a house, there is a road. The road leads to the house, and the house is set on a piece of land. We can describe the size of the house (so many square or cubic feet), the size of the land (so many acres), and the length of the road (so many miles). We could even analyze the ratio of one measurement to another if we found that useful; that would be a kind of analysis in that it would show a relationship among the different objects. Another kind would be a map where objects are placed spatially in relation to one another.

When we try to dissect human experience this way, we run into trouble. We have spoken of "society." Where is it? Can you photograph society as you photograph the house, road, or land? You could photograph some of its leaders and followers, its sites and symbols, but could you photograph "it"? "Culture" is even more difficult to grasp concretely, for culture is not a physical thing but an attitude, a way of viewing the world. We can describe indications of a certain cultural pattern – people hurrying or loitering as clues to their assumptions about time, for example – but culture itself is an abstraction that we make based on such indications. There is nothing wrong with an abstraction so long as we recognize it for what it is. But inevitably we are tempted to treat the abstraction as a thing. This is what Alfred North Whitehead called the "fallacy of misplaced concreteness," that is, to mistake an abstraction for a concrete thing[19] – to imagine that culture and society, say, are like two boxes that we could move around and stack on top of each other. When we differentiate experience into categories, we must remember that is what they are – categories, constructed by us, the analysts.

Gregory Bateson, in reflecting on his efforts at differentiating a certain New Guinea way of life into categories, emphasized this point:

> I found I had given no clear criterion for discriminating the elements of culture which I would pigeon-hole as ethos from those which I would pigeon-hole as structure or pragmatic function. I began to doubt the validity of my categories and performed an experiment.
> ...I drew a lattice of nine squares on a large piece of paper, three rows of squares with three squares in each row. I labelled the hor-

izontal rows with my bits of culture and the vertical columns with
my categories. Then I forced myself to see each bit as conceivably
belonging to each category. I found that it could be done.[20]

Bateson concluded:

> It is instructive too to perform the same experiment with such con-
> cepts as economics, kinship and land tenure, and even religion, lan-
> guage, and "sexual life" do not stand too surely as categories of
> behavior, but tend to resolve themselves into labels for points of
> view from which all behavior may be seen.[21]

It is not just in the social sciences that analysts make analytical
distinctions. Physical scientists do so as well. This is obvious with
respect to such categories as atoms and molecules, but true also of
the most familiar categories we use to perceive the physical world.
Take height and weight. A box can be characterized in terms of
weight and height, but these descriptive measurements are no more
intrinsic to the box than are the categories of culture and society
intrinsic to our experience. In each case, analysts make distinctions
that are more or less useful, depending on the task or question at
issue, in characterizing the reality that we wish to construct, discover, or describe.

The point is simple yet elusive. Perhaps a silly example will help
us remember it. A German nursery song goes like this:

> Mein Hut, der hat drei Ecken.
> Drei Ecken hat mein Hut.
> (My Hat, it has three corners.
> Three corners, my hat has.)

The song concludes, "Und hat er nicht drei Ecken, dann ist es nicht
mein Hut!" ("If my hat did not have three corners, it would not
be my hat!") Nonsense? Yes, but the song illustrates the identifi-
cation of a thing by its attributes. The owner of the hat identifies
it by its three corners. This is fallacious, for the hat also has many
other attributes – color, shape, and so on. One can never completely
describe anything, for one can always abstract more attributes. The
attributes are not the thing.

In the same way, to describe human experience as having cultural,
social, psychological, political, economic, biological, or physical
attributes is not to describe completely that experience. Each at-

tribute is simply one aspect, abstracted by the analyst to highlight some particular characteristic.

For centuries questions regarding the reality of attributes have haunted scientists and philosophers. Democritus wrote twenty-three centuries ago: "Sweet and bitter, cold and warm as well as all the colors, all these things exist but in opinion and not in reality; what really exists are unchangeable particles, atoms, and their motions in empty space."[22] Speaking of sensuous qualities like color, smell, taste, and sound, Galileo said that "they can no more be ascribed to the external objects than can the tickling or the pain caused sometimes by touching such objects."[23]

John Locke tried to distinguish between primary qualities of geometrical shape inherent in the thing itself and the properties that were projections of sense organs.[24] The artificial nature of this distinction was evident to later thinkers. Leibniz, the German mathematician, for example, wrote that "not only light, color, heat, and the like, but motion, shape and extension too are mere apparent qualities."[25]

Gradually, some philosophers and scientists concluded that the whole objective universe of matter and energy, atoms and stars, exists only as a construction of consciousness. Berkeley put it this way:

> All the choirs of heaven and furniture of earth, in a word all those bodies which compose the mighty frame of the world, have not any substance without the mind. . . . So long as they are not actually perceived by me, or do not exist in my mind, or that of any other created spirit, they must either have no existence at all, or else subsist in the mind of some Eternal Spirit.[26]

But Einstein took this kind of thinking farther. In Einstein's thought even space and time are forms of intuition that cannot be divorced from consciousness: "Space has no objective reality except as an order or arrangement of the objects we perceive in it, and time has no independent existence apart from the order of events by which we measure it."[27]

If, then, "physical reality" is a subjective category that we construct, how much more is our perception of human experience dependent on the concepts we employ to construct it?

Anthropology, then, favors perceptions of wholes. Yet it is necessary to differentiate wholes into categories. But it is essential, too, to remind ourselves that any such category is only that, not "reality."

Culture and experience
To say that the concept of "culture" is an abstraction is not to say that the attitudes, beliefs, and other dispositions that humans manifest and that we categorize under the label "culture" are not real; these human dispositions are real enough in our experience.

To sum up, again: Anthropology teaches several lessons, which may seem contradictory but in fact are interrelated. The first lesson is holism, that we should try to view wholes. The second is that, try as we might, we cannot succeed in grasping the whole, hence we must distinguish categories. The third is that we must guard against concretizing any category into a thing; we must always remember that it is simply an abstraction from the whole. But the fourth lesson is that, in avoiding the fallacy of misplaced concreteness, we should not commit the fallacy of misplaced abstractness; our label for a phenomenon is an abstraction, but that phenomenon can nonetheless have reality and power in experience.

We now place culture in some of the experiential contexts that have made it central and salient in anthropology.

The concept of culture in relation to nature
Who smells the worse, men or dogs? The answer to this riddle turns on the way "smells" is used. If in the active sense of smelling as a way of sensing, then dogs are the best; they are better smellers. If "smell" is intended as a quality imputed to the creature by an observer, then we cannot answer the question without asking, "According to whom?" The popular stereotype in our culture, at least in some circles, is that dogs smell worse than men, but some dog lovers might disagree, or careful observers might say it depends on who bathed most recently. And some cultures might idealize dog scent as we do the scent of roses. Here a pun on "smell" leads us from the seemingly objective observations of nature reported by physical anthropology or conventional wisdom (dogs and other lower mammals with long snouts perform better at olfaction than do the higher primates, including men, whose olfactory apparatus has reduced through evolution) to the world of shared subjectivity, which is to say, culture: Which group holds what opinion about

the scent of dogs versus that of men? The question suggests a distinction between nature and culture, but it also reminds us that the two are associated, in that cultures formulate opinions about nature.

The distinction between culture and nature has an important but complex history in anthropology and Western civilization; a brief summary will be useful.

Roots in Western civilization

The Greeks instilled a profound dualism in Western thought. Distinctions between mind and body, form and substance, thoroughly penetrated Western thinking for centuries. Within this dualistic framework, the Romans developed a notion of "nature" as the basic qualities inherent in a thing. This meaning was extended until "nature" became a self-contained material world. The groundwork was laid for our modern notions of natural science and also for a notion of what is not-nature (later named "culture").

Greek dualism was in sharp contrast to the Hebrew notion of creation. The Hebrews saw the world as an arena for the activity of God, Yahweh, so that the idea of a "closed" material world separate from a nonmaterial spiritual world was foreign to them. Nevertheless, the Hebrews contributed to the idea of culture. In their view of creation, man was made "in the image of God" and given dominion over the earth. The human was distinguished from the nonhuman. The Book of Genesis addressed not only the important philosophical question "Why is there something rather than nothing at all?" (it was Yahweh who created matter, i.e., the heavens and the earth); Genesis also addressed the questions "Why is there life instead of simply nonlife?" (it was Yahweh that breathed in the breath of life) and "Why is there consciousness and not simply nonconscious activity?" (the distinction between human and animal existence in Yahweh's creation and the transition from Eden to the "real world"). Or to restate the final question, "Why is there culture and not simply nature?"

The separation of culture from nature in anthropology

Although the concept of culture as distinct from nature is grounded in Judaic and Greek tradition, elaborated by centuries of Western philosophical and theological thought, it also has a recent history within anthropology and other social sciences. Stated briefly, this history involves the concepts of race, gender, and instinct. On the whole, anthropology and other social sciences have rejected explanations that assume such biological or pseudobiological causes as race, gender, and instinct and have emphasized instead social and cultural factors. In fact, the invention and development of the concept of culture are in part an attempt to explain behavioral differences where the natural (racial, gender, or instinctual) explanations failed.

During the colonial period, when Western nations ruled much of Africa and Asia, it was common to refer to colonized groups as "races" different from the colonizing group, and to attribute to each group qualities allegedly stemming from its race. Westerners spoke of the "African race" or the "Malay race" as a biologically defined group possessing such qualities as laziness or a happy-go-lucky attitude that were part of their genetic makeup. The world was divided into black, brown, yellow, red, and white races, and within each category finer distinctions were made – for example, within the white category between Celtic, Teutonic, and Slavic "races." Qualities of behavior were attributed to racial subtype – among Celts, one spoke of the dour Scot versus the talkative Irish. Even the particularities of individual behaviors were often explained by racial heritage. The *Dictionary of American Biography*, for example, includes the following about the life of one well-known American author, William Dean Howells: "His ancestry was mixed, a Welsh ingredient predominating strongly on his father's side, and a Pennsylvania German on his mother's. An English great-grandmother sobered the Welsh ferment; an Irish grandfather (mother's father) aerated the Teutonic phlegm."[28]

This racial way of thinking reached its peak in the nineteenth and early twentieth centuries, but it is by no means dead. Racism is rife throughout the world, whether among American whites describing blacks; Australians, the Aborigines; Chinese, the Malays; or Hindu brahmins, the "untouchables." The racial mode of explanation appears constantly and innocently in popular culture. A recent issue of *TV Guide*, for example, explains the personality of singer Crystal Gayle as being due to "Cherokee Indian and Irish blood coursing through her veins."[29] On a recent television program, a well-known commentator displayed a familiar racial bias in the very act of protesting racial bias; she stated that early movies showed jaundiced portrayals of members of the "Jewish race." Apparently she did not realize that Judaism is a religious and cultural category rather than a racial one, because it includes representatives of a variety of physical types.

Like race, gender qualities were considered genetic. In Victorian ideology, men were strong, dominant, and assertive; women – the "fair sex" – submissive and delicate. Accordingly, men should stride out into the world to conquer, women should confine themselves to the home. Because the qualities of each gender were assumed to be given genetically, change, through upbringing or education, was considered negligible.

The notion of "instinct" attributed to genetic heritage the behaviors of all persons, whatever their gender or group membership. If someone was altruistic or selfish, aggressive or passive, brave or cowardly, such behaviors were explained as instinct – a behavioral disposition given genetically at birth, rather than learned through experience.

The problem with such grossly simple genetic explanations was that they failed to account for obvious facts. What if an African or Malay went to Oxford and came away with behavior, speech, and even mode of thought more British than African or Malay? What if a woman like Nancy Astor, the outspoken Virginian who was the first woman elected to the British Parliament, shattered stereotypes of the womanly role? What if, as numerous psychological experiments demonstrated, learning could override or modify inherited tendencies? (For example, comparisons of identical twins separated at birth demonstrated that despite shared heredity, their different experiences could markedly affect personality, intelligence, and even physical characteristics.)

Cross-cultural anthropological studies provided a kind of natural laboratory through which to sort out nature and nurture, provocatively if not conclusively. Margaret Mead's studies of the Arapesh, Tjambuli, and Mundugumor tribes of New Guinea are examples. She showed that gender roles differed dramatically among the three tribes, although the genetic basis was presumably the same. In fact, among the Tjambuli, men formerly headhunters but now prevented from that occupation owing to law, had become, in their confined idleness, like the Western stereotype of women: spending their time primping and gossiping. The women were the sturdy, laconic, no-nonsense backbones of the tribe. Mead's conclusion – provocative if overstated – was that culture could modify gender roles markedly.[30]

In physical anthropology, the concept of race was challenged at several levels. Physical anthropologists argued that all peoples had a common origin, probably African, and that so-called racial variations were adaptations to varied environments (thus the lighter skins of northern Europeans and northern Asians came from thousands of years of living in comparatively sunless environments). In any case, the so-called racial differences were minor variations within a single species, not comparable to differences between species. In fact, the concept of "race" itself was discredited because physical features, whether visible (phenotypic) or measurable only through such techniques as blood-typing (genotypic), were distributed in a pattern too complex and ever-changing to be captured by the old race types or, indeed, any "racial typology." If the physical features attributed to various populations were not explained by the concept of race, so much less could behavioral and psychological characteristics be so explained.

Here, then, was a gap in explanation. The "natural" factors could not explain variations in behavior and way of life, so some other explanation was needed. Social sciences seized on social, economic, or psychological factors, and anthropology focused on "culture." Culture, as a pattern transmitted not genetically but by teaching and learning, could explain how Malays or Africans, males or females, or anyone else acted – and how they could change under changed circumstances. In fact, where earlier studies had emphasized the effect of biology on culture, some anthropological studies show the opposite (thus Boas showed that the so-called racial trait of head shape differed between Eastern European immigrants and their children, owing to the influence of the American setting).[31]

Structuralism
The pre–World War II studies previously mentioned strove to show how culture was a factor in behavior; they endeavored to factor out the cultural from the biological and to demonstrate the power

of culture to affect behavior and other attributes. After World War II, French anthropologist Claude Lévi-Strauss and others developed an approach that focused on culture as such, elucidating the logical patterning or "structure" of culture as an expression of universal proclivities of the human mind. This approach became known as structuralism.

This kind of patterning that structuralists found in culture is illustrated by a stoplight. A stoplight delineates only three meaningful categories (red, green, and yellow), in contrast to the spectrum of light frequencies found in nature, which is a continuum running the gamut of color in every shade and hue. Some stoplights may be darker green or brighter red than others, but these subtleties make no difference; it is the categories that matter. Culture is seen as imposing categories and order on natural continua. Culture is categorical, whereas nature is process – a flow lacking distinctions. The absolutism of culture is essential; categorical systems must be imposed on the chaos of the natural world, for only in this way is order given to an otherwise unordered existence.[32]

The structuralist approach is both a vision of the world and a way of analyzing it. Assuming that culture is a system of categories, structuralists proceed to lay bare such categories expressed in a variety of cultural systems: in language, in kinship, in mythology. In his earliest analysis of myth, for example, Claude Lévi-Strauss dissected the story of Oedipus. He divided all the episodes into two pairs of categories: stressed versus nonstressed kinship, and stressed versus nonstressed origins. Oedipus's killing of his father, for example, exemplifies nonstressed kinship while Oedipus's marrying his mother exemplifies stressed kinship – a rather coldly analytical way of categorizing highly traumatic events! Lévi-Strauss then shows how the myth resolves the contradictions between the categories.[33]

Structuralist analysis, then, is basically classification. One takes events such as episodes in a myth, then classifies them into categories. The dramatist might emphasize the way the Oedipus plot unfolds onstage, but the structuralist emphasizes the myth's way of classifying the world. In this way, the structuralist claims to reveal the structures of human thought.

The structuralist view of the relationship between culture and nature is most easily appreciated by applying it to some examples from our own culture.

Culture and nature as categories in folk, academic, and anthropological culture

Places to eat and places to sleep: the folk culture of the Jefferson Davis Highway. Driving south from Pittsboro, North Carolina, on Highway 15–501 (the Jefferson Davis Highway), I invited my children to play a game. They were asked to record the names of all lodging and eating places. After a hundred miles of this, we examined the two lists, which differed in a relevant way. No eating place had a name of nonhuman nature, whereas numerous sleeping places did: for example, the Shady Lawn Motel or the Whispering Pines Lodge. Conversely, no sleeping place had a first name of a person only, whereas numerous eating places did: for example, Hermie's Hotdogs or Rae's Cafe. (It should be noted that few of the national chains, such as Howard Johnson's, McDonald's, or Holiday Inn, were on this route at the time of observation; the pattern noted refers primarily to local names on this highway; however, the pattern seems to hold on other roads elsewhere, as the reader can check.)

What might this mean? Lévi-Strauss's structuralism as explicated in his book *The Raw and the Cooked* came to mind. "Raw," or uncooked, is associated with nature; and cooking, with culture. Extending the association, sociability is necessary for culture, thus the connection of first names and cooking implies "culture." Conversely, the lack of sociability implied by sleeping (which, after all, removes one from communication) plausibly fits with the lack of persons' first names in motels and thus with the "nature" imagery in these.

Has Lévi-Strauss, like an anthropological Johnny Appleseed, sown his categories along Highway 15–501? Have the owners of motels and truck stops met and agreed on a format of terminology? These silly speculations serve to emphasize that dichotomies such as that between nature and culture are pervasive in "our" culture (whether it be defined as Western, American, Judeo-Christian-Greco, or whatever) and therefore get expressed in regular patterns unintentionally but with striking regularity, as in these names of places to eat and places to sleep.

Academic culture: some places of science and learning. Universities and colleges name according to a variety of formats. Sometimes streets bear names of disciplines or methods, such as Logic Lane at Oxford or Philosophische Weg at Heidelberg; more often, however, they are named for persons (usually benefactors, although in the European universities one may find a few streets even named after scholars). Let us shift for the moment from names to spatial layout, asking how these exhibit the nature-culture distinction.

At my own university, the distinction is obvious and clear. The old campus (which was begun in 1793) is the site of the humanities and social sciences, as well as the administration offices and such professional schools as business and library science. As one moves away from the old toward the new, one comes upon the buildings and laboratories of the natural sciences, then the domain of health affairs: the medical school, school of public health, dentistry, pharmacy, and the hospital. Adjacent to this health and natural-science complex are the athletic facilities: gymnasiums, football stadium, and the like. Thus, "culture" is located in the old campus, "nature" in the new.

Something like this kind of arrangement characterizes many other universities or colleges as well. At Oxford University, for example, most of the oldest colleges, which tend to be humanistically oriented, are found in the area surrounding the Bodleian Library. As one moves out from this center, the structures of science and medicine become more prominent: for example, the engineering building, Wolfson College, the Radcliffe Infirmary, and, especially, the University Museum. This museum, built in the mid-nineteenth century as an edifice devoted to the rise of science of that day, was despised as violating the spirit of Oxford University by certain older, more religiously and humanistically inclined sectors.

Should one move beyond single campuses to consider university and college systems embracing multiple campuses, the basic nature-culture distinction continues to be manifest. For example, in America many states boast a duo of the major state university (often termed "the University of X State") plus a usually newer school (often termed "X State University"). The first is usually more fully developed in the liberal arts; the second, in engineering and agricultural studies. This is somewhat like the division in England between university and technical school, or in Germany between university and *Hochschule*. The division is, of course, obvious, but it serves to remind us how we perpetuate an arbitrary cultural and philosophical distinction through ramified designs, not only of each campus but of vast state systems as well.

Museums are generally thought of not as statements of philosophy but simply as collections of things. Yet their arrangement, too, manifests worldviews. The national museum for the United States of America, the Smithsonian Institution in Washington, D.C., places Western civilization in one section, such as the Museum of American History, whereas the exotic people of the world are placed in the Museum of *Natural* History, together with mollusks and dinosaurs.[34] Does not this express a conception – rather biased – of what is nature and what is culture?

These cases range from the tawdry, incidental, and popular symbolism of motels and eating joints along a highway to the edifices of academia: universities and museums. They illustrate several points.

The nature-culture distinction is analytical, yet manifested concretely. The distinction is couched abstractly, but helps order concrete, observable phenomena. It is not, of course, perfect in its fit, and some facts do not fit. Thus, for example, the distinction between females and males is frequently allied to that between nature and culture. Women have traditionally been linked to birth, nurturance, and food-gathering; men, to governance, priesthood, and high technology, speaking broadly and thinking of a range of world societies. Yet people buck some categories, and perhaps will refute them. At Oxford, the women's colleges are generally located in the "science" area, yet "science" is traditionally more a man's game, so here women appear to be located ambiguously, reflecting perhaps nothing more than the historical fact that the women's colleges and the science buildings both arrived late on campus. Structuralist distinctions like "culture" and "nature" serve to order observations only to a point, then are best abandoned.

Or, perhaps better, they can be refined. For instance, to what degree does the distinction between culture and nature illuminate institutional arrangements in non-Western societies? What is one

to make of the suggestive (but perhaps accidental) fact that in Surabaya, Indonesia, the Office of Culture (Kantor Kebudayaan) is
placed across the street from the city zoo? Is this parallel to the city
of Edinburgh's placing its modern art museum in the midst of its
botanical garden? A Lévi-Straussian could probably construe from
such instances a pattern showing nineteenth-century efforts at si-
multaneously domesticating the natural creative impulses of people
and the plant and animal worlds, especially in their tropical man-
ifestations (the Edinburgh greenhouse features palm trees). Such
queries, idle and incidental in some ways, nevertheless lead toward
perception of pattern, and show that the structuralist approach and
the nature-culture distinction are at least suggestive at many levels.

Anthropological culture: evolution and other theories. So far, we
have viewed the distinction between nature and culture as embodied
in "folk categories," beginning with a humble country highway and
ending with the university. If we move from "folk" to "academic"
theories, we find the same distinction. Consider the following
"facts" or "theories," that is, portrayals, of human evolution, which
are standard in textbooks of anthropology.

The sequence runs from hominoid to hominid, that is, from ancestors of both apes and humans to ancestors of humans only, finally
to humans themselves. Specifically, evolution is seen moving
through phases, from various hominoids, to *Australopithecus*, to
Homo erectus, and to *Homo sapiens*. Separated by a time of approximately one million years between each phase, evolution passed
from legs, to tools, to brain: *Australopithecus* had humanlike bi-
pedal posture and gait, but a very small brain (approximately 500
cc., or one-third the size of the modern brain); *Homo erectus* had
bipedality and tools, that is, material culture permitted by freeing
the hands through bipedality; and finally, *Homo sapiens* had a large
brain, which permitted language and symbols.

This reconstruction is based partly on archaeological and physical
anthropological excavation, while a second but related analysis is
based on observing living nonhuman primates: chimpanzees,
baboons, gorillas, orangutans, lemurs, and so forth. The two
analyses use similar distinctions. Analogous to distinguishing tool-
using and language-using phases of hominid evolution from prior
"precultural" phases, one tries to distinguish humans from other

primates, according to whether they do or do not use tools and language. At one time, the distinction was considered absolute: They did not; we did. More recently, both linguistic and nascent tool-using capacities have been discovered in certain primates (e.g., pygmy chimpanzees can manipulate symbols in the fashion of language, and chimps use a stick to dig up termites); but the distinction is still considered valid in a relative sense.

A related comparison, between the periods of gestation and maturation for human and nonhuman primates, shows neatly that, as one moves up the evolutionary "scale," the duration of gestation and maturation increases. This suggests that humans depend more on learning whereas lower primates depend more on instinct.

Here, then, are parallel comparisons: between earlier and later phases of evolution, which is to say, less human versus more human types, and between lower and higher primates, again between less human and more human traits. In these comparisons, less human versus more human are associated with less culture versus more, in the form of language and tools; language and tools are associated, in turn, with large brains; and large brains are associated with long periods of dependency during gestation and maturation, which permit learning. The nature-culture distinction underlies all of these comparisons.

Evolution after the advent of *Homo sapiens* is typically seen as passing through a lengthy phase of hunting and gathering (the characteristic human pattern for several million years) to a phase of farming and pastoralism, then to industrialization. Once crops and animals were domesticated, civilization evolved, which meant cities and states, literacy, class hierarchies, bureaucracies, and other accoutrements of "culture." Here humankind is seen as passing from a more "natural" phase to one in which nature is domesticated. Finally, with recent industrialization, the only jungle left is asphalt, and humans are alienated from nature.

Studies comparing contemporary primates and humans parallel evolutionary studies. Thus, contemporary hunting and gathering or agricultural societies are analyzed and compared with ancient ones. The comparisons are not so crude as those once made between "us" and the *Naturvölker* ("natural man"), but the nature-culture distinction is still prominently implied.

The point here is not to criticize these evolutionary reconstructions and comparisons, which are, in fact, impressively clear, comprehensive, and convincing. The point is simply to indicate that in academic, indeed, anthropological, theory as well as in folk imagery, the nature versus culture distinction is prominent.

Turning from reconstructions of biological and cultural evolution, which are the focuses of physical anthropology and archaeology, to the patterning of contemporary life, which is the focus of cultural and social anthropology, the nature-culture distinction remains elemental. Many of the most fundamental discoveries of early social and cultural anthropology entailed distinguishing these two categories, which formerly had been confused.

Early anthropologists demonstrated the need to distinguish the cultural from the natural and were able to show that traits assumed to be natural might in fact be cultural. Later, this kind of distinction was at the base of disciplinary breakthroughs. Social anthropologists realized that kinship relationships as defined in the society were not the same as biological relations grounded in reproduction. Linguists realized that units of sound in speech as defined by the culture (phonemes) were not the same as units of sound defined by physics and anatomy. When anthropologists and linguists recognized such a distinction between physical and cultural realities, they were better able to render precise analyses, whether of kinship or of language. Out of this grew structuralism, with its focus on the structure of culture as such – whether manifested in language, myth, or general schemata of classification such as that nature-culture classification we are discussing now.

Whatever the validity of anthropological theories – evolutionary, structuralist, or otherwise – it is clear that in anthropology, as in folk culture, the relationship between nature and culture is pivotal. "Culture" and "nature" are seen as essential aspects of human experience, the one grounded in, yet distinct from, the other.

Society

Culture does not float in a vacuum; it is sustained by persons who are members of society. The understandings that constitute culture exist only when they are shared by persons whose relationships constitute some kind of organized system.

The way that culture is organized has been characterized as logicomeaningful, in contrast to the "causal-functional" organization of society:

> By logico-meaningful integration, characteristic of culture, is meant the "sort of" integration one finds in a Bach fugue, in Catholic dogma, or in the general theory of relativity; it is a unity of style, of logical implication, of meaning and value. By causal-functional integration, characteristic of the social system, is meant the kind of integration one finds in an organism, where all the parts are united in a single causal web; each part is an element in a reverberating causal ring which "keeps the system going."[35]

A cultural system can be envisioned as a set of major premises – similar to a philosophical, theological, or legal system – from which its more specific minor premises can be derived. Thus, from the notion that "there is one God and He is all powerful," as in Islam, Judaism, or Christianity, derive more particular points, such as mistrust of animism (which locates spiritual power not in a single being but in many), or dilemmas (such as how a God could create evil, if He is both good and all powerful). Such elements are connected in a more or less logical way and could be diagramed as a chart showing the major premises at the top and minor ones fanning out toward the bottom. Less formal cultural patterns, such as views of time and classifications of nature and culture, show something like this logical structure, too, though less neatly.

The causal-functional system is envisioned as a ring of arrows, rather like an English "roundabout," a circuit diagram, a flow chart, or a circulatory system. Each unit or node in the flowing process is both cause of the one in front and effect of the one behind. A social system such as a bureaucracy has this form; in a university bureaucracy, for example, students pay tuition, which is a condition for their registering; they register as a condition of signing up for courses; they take courses to graduate. One thing leads to another in a more or less systematic cause-effect process.

If the school of thought in anthropology most geared to reveal the logicomeaningful patterning of culture is *structuralism*, that most clearly oriented to trace the causal-functional character of society is *functionalism*. Functionalism analyzes society as if it were a machine – a set of working parts, a functioning system. Structuralism and functionalism are not absolutely separate. They usefully complement each other. Each views life from a different perspective, but both are holistic — they try to see wholes.

Although anthropology is concerned generally with society, it has a special interest in one kind of society, the small community.

The small community

The scope of anthropology is vast. It treats the "cradles" of civilization, the great historic civilizations, and contemporary life — sharing, of course, these topics with other fields. But the most distinctive focus of anthropology is on a kind of group that at first glance seems to relegate the field to obscurity and eventual extinction: the exotic and the small. Anthropology seeks to know the nature of the elementary human community. We shall first try to discover the category, folk community, in folklore. Consider these simple anecdotes:

1. A French peasant woman once went to church in a neighboring village. She did not laugh at the pastor's jokes. Asked why not, she replied, "It is not my village."

2. A man from a small town called Hampton told his friend that he was about to marry a certain woman. "But she's slept with everybody in Hampton!" exclaimed the friend. "Hell, Hampton ain't no big town!" retorted the man.

3. A mountaineer from Appalachia once left home and, in order to ensure his sweetheart's undying affection, wrote her daily. The result was that she married the postman.

What can these tales be taken to illustrate?

The first demonstrates the strength of group identity. So strong is that sense that the peasant woman refuses even to know or perceive a message from another group; here knowledge is grounded in community — Durkheim's thesis.

The second could be interpreted as follows: The traditional concept of virginity is absolute, all or nothing, so that a single sexual episode destroys virginity. "Hampton ain't no big town" makes a more slippery argument, that virginity and purity are more a matter of degree, so that sleeping with a hundred is not as bad as sleeping with a thousand. The tale juxtaposes the quantitative norm that is at the base of contemporary society with the absolute and categorical, which is at the base of traditionalism.

The third anecdote exemplifies the power of the face-to-face as opposed to the distant relationship. The letter, sent through the bureaucratic channel of the post office, cannot match direct contact — another quality considered at the center of the true "community."

In sum, these little fables illustrate group identity, categorical norms, and the power of face-to-face relationships. All of these features are attributed to the authentic community, which social sciences sometimes term a *Gemeinschaft*, or "folk society," to use the German word introduced by sociologist Ferdinand Tönnies.[36]

Through most of human evolution, such a small community has been the basis of human life and for this reason is of special interest in anthropology's effort at discerning that which is basic. Even though anthropology has branched into the study of the broadest and most complex social systems, it retains a focus on the small community. Anthropologists continue to do research among the few surviving hunting and gathering groups, such as the African Bushmen, the Australian Aborigines, and the jungle tribes of Borneo. They also do fieldwork in peasant villages in India, Mexico, or Afghanistan and France; in urban, ethnically integrated neighborhoods in Hong Kong or London; in communes, such as the Israeli kibbutz or Amish and Hutterite communities; within religious sects and other cultural movements that display communal attributes; and within such institutions as hospitals or factories treated as small groups. Thus, while branching out into a variety of social settings, anthropology has retained its classic focus on the communal group.

The branch of anthropology most intensely focused on this kind of social life is known as social anthropology, and it traces its inspiration especially to the French social philosopher mentioned earlier, Emile Durkheim. An important source was Durkheim's 1893 doctoral dissertation, *The Division of Labor in Society*, in which he set forth the distinction between "mechanical" and "organic" solidarity.[37] Organic solidarity characterizes contemporary, urbanized society like our own. Here connections are based on division of labor: The butcher exchanges his meat for money, the baker exchanges his bread for money, and with that money the butcher can buy bread and the baker, meat. Each does his own work, and mutually useful exchange is what holds the society together. Mechanical solidarity is, according to Durkheim, found in traditional communities. Unity does not come from division of labor and economic exchange. Instead, everyone works at the same thing, and unity is based on shared morality, a firm commitment to a single norm and belief. In such a "moral community," social relationships are fixed and rigid, grounded in kinship, rather than flexible in the manner of contractual relationships that adapt to needs of the marketplace.

In social anthropology the patterning of so-called mechanical societies – the small communities – has been analyzed everywhere in the world. It has become clear that such communities are not so "mechanical" as Durkheim supposed. Systems of social relationships function in unbelievably complex and subtle ways, and free choice has considerable play. Yet anthropology continues to affirm that such communities sustain a strong solidarity, especially in comparison with our own society. Three well-known examples will suffice.

Max Gluckman's theory of multiplex social relationships. Max Gluckman has characterized relationships in traditional societies as "multiplex," by which is meant that every relationship includes many levels and aspects.[38] One's cousin is also one's co-worker, neighbor, teacher, chief, and father-in-law. A community based on such multiplex social relationships is like a net of inextricably tangled thick ropes. In such a community, the social order is heavy and all-encompassing, in a way too profound for those of us who have never experienced it to imagine. Unity and harmony in such a group are a powerful experience, but conflict is equally powerful; disturbance in any rope sends shivers through the whole net. It is this multiplexity that causes conflict to become so pervasive that it spills out of the social into natural and supernatural realms; people believe that conflict wrecks crops and health and sends spirits into uproar. To restore order in the midst of such ramified disorder requires powerful ritual that enacts a unity of social relationships equal in multiplexity to the disunity.

Mary Douglas's theory of grid and group. Douglas distinguishes two dimensions of group communal life: the internal (*grid*, which is the network that binds and classifies persons in relation to one another) and the external (*group*, the community's identity contrasted to those outside its boundaries).[39] She then classifies communities according to how these two dimensions combine. In the classic *Gemeinschaft*, both group and grid are strong. In our kind of society, both are weak. An archaic society such as classical Greece is weak in grid but strong in group, for the Greek sense of an ingroup identity against outsiders was strong. Other societies show the reverse emphasis, with strong grid (as in networks of trade and political teamwork) but weak identity of ingroup as opposed to outgroup.

Having established a typology of social patterns, Douglas then shows how experiences and cultures correlate with each type. The strong group–strong grid community musters rituals that fortify faith and solidify society, whereas the weak group–weak grid community (if one may use the word) cannot. Strong group–weak grid societies emphasize such practices as witchcraft and sorcery that project a strong sense of social boundary onto the physical body; members of such societies worry about noxious substances crossing those boundaries and harming the body. The weak group–strong grid type is prone to religious movements that mobilize "grid" networks around prophetic leaders.

Victor Turner's theory of communitas. Turner rings yet another change on the Durkheimian framework. Where Durkheim emphasizes the established structures of group life, Turner emphasizes what he terms "anti-structure."[40] Anti-structure, for example, is found in the "liminal" state in which initiates are suspended as they pass from childhood to adulthood in rites of passage. Initiates are neither child nor adult, they are "betwixt and between" these established statuses. Yet in this "liminal" state, the initiates enjoy that unity and fellowship which comes from shared suffering; "misery loves company" during hazing, torture, and other hardships. Turner shows, then, a *communitas* that flourishes in the "liminal" interstices of society, outside and in between the established structures.

Gluckman, Douglas, and Turner all affirm the strength of community life, how the tightly knit, thickly braided entanglements of the small group sustain a strong unity. No purely "mechanical" society can exist, for humans are too plastic, creative, and ornery; but social anthropology brings home to us how social relationships function in their interlocking, mutually reinforcing ways to sustain the community.

Not only are communities envisioned by these social anthropologists as tightly knit and thickly textured. Such communities also embrace culture. Gluckman, Douglas, and Turner all emphasize how they are embodied in ritual; ritual sustains belief, and belief is part of culture. These models of community illustrate a distinctive conviction of anthropology, that the small community is a site and source of culture.

The exotic location of community and culture

Western and Westernized cultures hold dual visions of cities. On the one side, the city is glittering steel and glass: technological marvels and sophistication. Everything was up-to-date in Kansas City, marveled country folk in *Oklahoma* as they celebrated the newfangled urban technology. Still in the positive vein, the city is a place of exciting entertainment and fun; the relevant lyrics are "How you gonna keep 'em down on the farm, after they've seen Paris!" On the negative side, the city is sweatshops, tenements, and cauldrons of crime, an "asphalt jungle." These are the images introduced by writers like Charles Dickens and Emile Zola and celebrated daily by media accounts of muggings and rapes, drugs and poverty. Even for the privileged, city life may represent only the gray flannel suit and the heartless corporate bureaucracy that crushes human creativity, kindness, and passion. Nor are these images confined entirely to the Western nations; parallels are easy to find for Asian or African cities, such as Jakarta or Tokyo, or Cairo or Nairobi.

Contrasted to the pressures and deprivations of urban life i nature, advertised in colorful holiday travel brochures. Sunn' beaches, grassy fields, and colorful gardens promise relaxation while rugged mountains and crashing surf suggest excitement. Such scenes of the outdoors are always balanced by pictures of luxury hotels boasting bars, swimming pools, discotheques, and splendid dining rooms. Where are these holiday sites? Many are in the supposedly less "spoiled" areas of the industrial world: Scotland, Wales, the Cornish coast of England; Florida, the Rockies, Smokies, and Sierras; the Black Forest and the Alps. Again, parallels are found for non-Western urbanites: Malang and Bali or Lake Toba for Jakartans, for example, or Atami for Japanese city dwellers. Then, of course, the jet set of the First World have their favorite retreats in the Third World: Tahiti, the Caribbean, Mexico, and North Africa – just about anywhere that combines scenery and climate with comfortable accommodations.

Popular culture depicts these getaway places as nature; they are sunshine, snow, and flowers, or rocks and sea. Onto them is imposed Western culture only in the technological sense, so as to ensure comfort and convenience: plumbing, heating, air conditioning, luxurious beds and cafés, credit cards, airplanes, and buses or automobiles. What may exist of local culture is depicted, if at all, only in the fashion of trinkets, to be bought or viewed between dips in the pool and drinks in the bar: the ruins of Carthage or Crete seen through windows of air-conditioned buses, the folk dances displayed in the hotel lobby, the colorful costumes on exhibit in the museum or gift ship. Certainly no sustained engagement in the local culture is promised (or threatened) as part of the holiday package, for that would destroy the entire organization of the trip and violate its point, which is not to get involved but to get away from it all. Defined as object for detached viewing, local culture thus assumes a role, for the tourist, comparable to that of objects of nature: the rocks, trees, sea, and scenery; culture is merely a bit of local color.

In these matters, anthropology and popular culture are directly at odds. Popular culture considers that *we* are culture, that culture is located among us, the literate, urban moderns, and that nature is somewhere out there, away from the cities and towns in the exotic and unspoiled places. Tourists, even the more serious adventurers, get away from culture by fleeing to this nature.

Anthropologists, far from fleeing culture in their forays in the exotic, perversely seek it, in those places out there. Rather than restrict their engagement with the locals to a view of folk dances in the hotel, anthropologists endeavor to enter the community, to become engaged in it for months and years, to penetrate deeply the local culture, and, finally, to discover meaning.

Now, insofar as anthropologists find meaning in the exotic, does it follow that they cease to find meaning in the familiar? Is the anthropologists' search for meaning outside their culture a sign of their dislocation within it? There is truth in this. Anthropologists have been among those critical of the urbanized, large-scale society, while praising the virtues of the small folk community. Anthropologists, along with others, have pointed to the alienation and despair in modern society, the dreary abode of the "homeless mind." These criticisms take many forms, but one is this, that the sheer technological sophistication of modern, urban society renders it a kind of natural system by default; it is organized technically, by means and ends, rather than culturally, by meaning, hence it is meaningless. In this sense, the exotic small community, lacking technology but more deeply grounded in culture, is more meaningful.

The anthropological attitude is, in actuality, more complex than this. Like business people, doctors, computer programmers, or real estate agents, anthropologists hold their professional meetings in large hotels and fly in airplanes, paying with credit cards. Like everyone else in their home societies, most anthropologists are enmeshed in modernity; only a few have settled on distant isles. What is at issue, though, is not the actual life-style of individual anthropologists but the thrust and implication of the anthropological perspective, the focus of the anthropological lens. In choosing the exotic as a place to seek culture and meaning, a tendency is reinforced to regard as meaningless our own culture.

To summarize, one could argue as follows: If (1) anthropology identifies its favorite object of study as culture and opposes this to nature, and (2) anthropology also identifies its favored object of study as the exotic small community, while opposing this to Western or Westernized and urbanized society, then by simple associational logic the exotic small community is placed in relationship to culture – the two sharing the attribute of being the favored object of study – while the local urbanized society is linked to a notion of wasteland bereft of culture (and therefore in some sense merely nature: a loveless chaos lacking order or meaning).

Again, this formula is too simple. It applies a kind of structuralism to highlight tendencies in anthropological thought and imagery; the actualities are more complex. But the pattern has a foothold in the discipline and finds expression in various guises.

Culture and community in relation to individual and meaning

A group of physicians once asked me to discuss with them "the ethnographic method," as part of a study of techniques of observation that might enhance physicians' sensitivity to behavior of their patients. We carried out a brief exercise – a bit of "fieldwork" – which entailed observing the admissions area of a large hospital. The physicians were keen observers. Their reports emphasized certain aspects, however, and ignored others. They concentrated on individual behavior while ignoring cultural patterns. One physician, for example, wrote a detailed account of a child's tantrum, another described the frustrated response of a person attempting to get through the red tape of admissions. My own report emphasized the cultural assumptions embedded in the total setting of the admissions system; I noted, for example, that patients were directed to one area for cardiology, another for neurology, yet another for orthopedics – a pattern that reflects an assumption taken for granted in our biomedical worldview to the effect that the self is divisible into different elements – the heart, the brain, the limbs, and so on. The difference in the reports perhaps reflected a difference between anthropology and medicine: the one focusing more on the collective, shared cultural framework; the other, on the individual.

Because of its cultural and social focus, anthropology may seem to ignore the individual. In fact, some anthropological analyses are exquisitely revealing of individual characteristics; but the discipline encourages anthropologists to see individuals as representative of their society and culture. Let us consider some approaches to this relationship.

Anthropology affirms studies in social psychology that demonstrate the power of the group to influence personal experience. Experiments have shown, for example, that group pressure can persuade the person actually to violate his own perception of physical reality. A person is asked to state which of several lines on a board is longest, then he hears the opinion of some others, who have been instructed to agree on an erroneous judgment. The person usually changes his own correct estimate to conform to the erroneous group opinion.[41] Other studies show how the group can determine the rate at which a person works. Women assembling electrical devices would informally set certain limits on rates of work, and any "rate buster" would be ostracized. Eventually, that person would conform, even if she could easily go faster and make more money.[42] A third study shows that the extraordinarily high morale of German troops during World War II was not fanatical loyalty to Naziism but cohesion and loyalty to the small military group in which the individual became embedded. The German army kept each small unit intact throughout the war, instead of transferring individuals among units. As a result, the members developed an intense sense of comradeship that overrode danger and discomfort. (For a fictional portrayal of this pattern, see Erich Maria Remarque's *All Quiet on the Western Front*.)[43]

These social psychological studies are striking in that they show how the group can influence the individual even in a Western cultural setting premised on individualism. Even more striking is the power of the group in societies with a more collectivist cultural framework. Victor Turner's description of a ritual healing among the Ndembu of Africa, for example, shows how in a few hours of ritual a person was healed of psychosomatic maladies that modern psychotherapy would treat through months and years. The secret was simply that, in the course of the intense and absorbing rite, the group that had given rise to the maladies by rejecting the patient now accepted him; and this acceptance was immensely more meaningful than would be possible in modern life because of the total embeddedness of the patient's existence in this multiplex group.[44]

So much for studies that demonstrate the sheer force of group membership on the psyche. What of the relationship between the individual and culture? Anthropology designates this field as "culture and personality," a few findings of which should be noted.

The theoretical inspiration for this field came mainly from the psychoanalytical psychology and psychiatry of Sigmund Freud. Following the Freudian emphasis on childhood experience as a determinant of the adult personality, the culture and personality studies focused especially on child rearing – the way it transmits cultural values and psychological dispositions to the individual. The Russian habit of swaddling, for example, was seen as reflecting and encouraging a national character prone to extremes of emotion.[45] The Balinese child's experience of its mother stimulating it then undercutting its aroused desire was seen as encouraging a withdrawn personality.[46] Training to be independent and self-reliant in American families was seen as encouraging self-blame, whereas a more collectivist attitude and setting instills a tendency to blame others.[47]

These kinds of relationships may sound simplistic and farfetched when summarized, but the detailed studies that are their basis are often ingenious and suggestive. However, they adopt from psychology and psychiatry a number of assumptions that anthropologists would question. One of these is the assumption that the individual, as a psychologically and culturally defined unit, is basically the same everywhere, and that differences stem primarily from differences in mode of child rearing through which culture has its impact. A more radical thesis, but also one more compatible with the anthropological perspective, is that culture and personality are not so easily distinguishable; that the very definition of who the person is, is cultural.

Consider again the premises of Western psychology and psychiatry. The individual is assumed to be a distinct unit, both synchronically and diachronically. Synchronically (at any given time), the personality is seen as a set of processes and structures attached to a single individual. Diachronically (that is, through time, as when one passes through the life cycle), the personality is seen as having continuity. These assumptions are illustrated by our saying, "I lead a life." We assume there is a distinct person, an "I"; that I *lead*, that I have some control over my existence, some autonomy and free will; and that the leading is of a *life*, by "life" implying an existence through time that is continuous, so that past experience influences present personality.

These assumptions are common. We make them every time we speak of careers, of biographies, of persons. They are part not only of our lay culture but of psychological and psychiatric theories. This is true regardless of school – Freudian, Jungian, behaviorist, developmental, or whatever – of psychology or psychiatry. Not only theories but also therapies are based on these assumptions – for example, psychoanalysis, which uncovers past traumas in order to explain and cure present neuroses.

These assumptions work adequately, most of the time, in cultures, like our own, that emphasize the distinctness of the self and the continuity of self through time. Other cultures do not necessarily hold these assumptions. In Java, for example, an individual often changes name when he changes status – from child to man, pilgrim to returnee, lesser rank to higher rank. The ease with which one changes name suggests that the Javanese place less emphasis on the continuity of individual identity through life than is customary in the West and place more emphasis on the matching of individual and social status. Another indication of this difference in emphasis is seen in the absence of biographical writing in classical Javanese culture and the character of much Javanese biographical writing done today; by comparison to Western biography, there is less attention to the process by which one experience leads to another as the subject's life unfolds and more emphasis on the cultural categories into which the subject fits. This kind of stamp by the culture on the very conception of the self – which may raise the question of whether "self" as we imagine it really exists in such situations – is emphasized in much of the recent anthropological inquiry into psychology and culture.

As anthropology turns to psychology, then, it sustains its dominant emphasis, which is on the cultural basis of human existence including the existence of the individual. Such an emphasis follows the logic of holism: to move from whole to part, from culture to society to individual, rather than the reverse.

Does anthropology, then, deny the existence of the individual? Is the individual imagined to be a robot, mechanically following the dictates of a cultural master? To the contrary, the individual is seen as free to choose and to act. But action is, as Max Weber emphasizes, always in terms of meaning;[48] and meaning comes from placement of one's acts in contexts, including culture. For anthropology, the individual is neither a robot nor an entirely independent self-willed little god but is a cultural individual – existing in freedom but also embodying that cultural mold in which he is cast in his particular society and historical epoch.

Overview

We have asked how anthropology sees reality in terms of its substantive concepts. We have argued that culture is the dominant concept, although it is seen holistically as part of a larger whole and analytically as an abstraction – a word, a category to label and conceptualize observations. Nevertheless, the aspect of human life we have called cultural has a reality and force that anthropology tries to demonstrate. We have tried to see how anthropology traces the ramifications of culture into social life and the life of the individual. To realize the force of culture is like realizing that our minds have an unconscious, that the earth is round or that it moves around the sun. That is, understanding and insight into our cultural grounding are powerfully revealing of the basis of our existence. To perpetuate this insight is the major substantive contribution of anthropology.

2

Method

If I be not deceived.
Primitive Baptist saying

E. E. Evans-Pritchard gives this account of his fieldwork among the
Nuer of Africa:

> Questions about customs were blocked by a technique I can com-
> mend to natives who are inconvenienced by the curiosity of eth-
> nologists. The following specimen of Nuer methods is the com-
> mencement of a conversation on the Nyanding river, on a subject
> which admits of some obscurity but, with willingness to co-operate,
> can soon be elucidated.
>
> *I*: Who are you?
> *Cuol*: A man.
> *I*: What is your name?
> *Cuol*: Do you want to know my *name*?
> *I*: Yes.
> *Cuol*: You want to know *my* name?
> *I*: Yes, you have come to visit me in my tent and I would like to
> know who you are.
> *Cuol*: All right. I am Cuol. What is your name?
> *I*: My name is Pritchard.
> *Cuol*: What is your father's name?
> *I*: My father's name is also Pritchard.
> *Cuol*: No, that cannot be true. You cannot have the same name as
> your father.
> *I*: It is the name of my lineage. What is the name of your lineage?
> *Cuol*: Do you want to know the name of my lineage?
> *I*: Yes.
> *Cuol*: What will you do with it if I tell you? Will you take it to your
> country?
> *I*: I don't want to do anything with it. I just want to know it since
> I am living at your camp.

Cuol: Oh well, we are Lou.

I: I did not ask you the name of your tribe. I know that. I am asking you the name of your lineage.

Cuol: Why do you want to know the name of my lineage?

I: I don't want to know it.

Cuol: Then why do you ask me for it? Give me some tobacco.

I defy the most patient ethnologist to make headway against this kind of opposition. One is just driven crazy by it. Indeed, after a few weeks of associating solely with Nuer one displays, if the pun be allowed, the most evident symptoms of "Nuerosis."[1]

A story is told of the Russian general Kutuzov. Before an important battle, his advisers were detailing high-level strategies. Bored, the old general slept. On the eve of the battle, he rode around and interviewed his sentries. In this way, it is said, he learned more about the actual situation than did his strategists.

This tale should appeal to the anthropologist. Like the old general, he distrusts abstract formulations distant from "real people" and "real life." He seeks truth from the natives in their habitat, by looking and listening. We call this "fieldwork."

Evans-Pritchard's account reminds us that inquiry is not so simple as the Kutuzov story suggests. We move now to comprehend this experience of fieldwork.

Travel

In the novel *Dr. Zhivago*, Boris Pasternak depicts a cultivated and privileged Moscow family, the Zhivagos, reduced by the Russian Revolution to clawing for survival. Foraging in the snow and ice for scraps of firewood, scavenging for food, Yurii Zhivago finally decides to move his wife, son, and wife's father away from their cherished urban life in Moscow to Siberia, where his wife's family has an old estate. Only by a hair do they get a seat on the crowded train – an achievement that requires Dr. Zhivago to squeeze the last favor from the collapsing order of which he has been an ambivalent part.

An endless train ride, made epic through sparse detail of place and time, is broken by marvelous adventures: notably Yurii's encounter with the ruthless Strelnikov, the teacher-become-soldier who moves about the country in an armored rail car stopping periodically to assassinate counterrevolutionaries. Captured, then set free after a curiously sympathetic interview (Strelnikov is the

husband of the woman, Lara, who later becomes Zhivago's lover),
Yurii is pulled back into the warmth of his family, now in a carriage
with a talkative Siberian lawyer whom Yurii senses will later serve
them strangely. They arrive at Torfianaia, where they board a wag-
on and are jolted through the countryside by a driver whose name
is that of a legendary blacksmith said to have equipped himself with
iron organs. Finally they reach the estate, now occupied by a farmer
whose family is amazed and discomfited to see them. They are at
journey's end, yet there is for them here *nothing*.

> The passengers got out, and Alexander Alexandrovich, hemming and
> hawing and taking off and putting on his hat, began to explain.
>   Their hosts were stuck dumb with amazement. Their genuine
> speechlessness lasted for several minutes; so did the sincere and ap-
> palled confusion of their miserable guests, who were burning with
> shame. The situation could not have been plainer, whatever might
> have been said.... Their painful embarrassment seemed to com-
> municate itself even to the mare, the foal, the golden rays of the
> setting sun, and the gnats that swarmed around Elena Proklovna
> and settled on her face and neck.
>   The silence was finally broken by Mikulitsyn. "I don't understand.
> I don't understand a thing and I never will. What do you think this
> is? The south, where the Whites are, and plenty of bread? Why did
> you pick on us? What on earth has brought you here – here, of all
> places?"[2]

Yet, in time, the farmer takes them into his house, and soon they
begin to homestead. Yurii falls into a routine of daily farm work
and cozy evenings around a stove. A few peasants become his patients, and, practical life established, he turns to more intellectual
quests. Riding three hours by horse to the town library, he writes
poems and studies the folklore and ethnology of the region. This
routine is destroyed eventually by his affair with Lara, which leads
ultimately to his death – the destiny of the romantic hero.

Order is best appreciated and cherished under conditions of disorder. Move to a new place – a new town, a new school, go off to
college. More radically, change cultures, as Zhivago did in traveling
to Siberia, and as an anthropologist would do in fieldwork. In a
radically new situation, life becomes what William James called
"booming, buzzing confusion," though the confusion may be empty
and silent rather than boom and buzz. In a foreign place, one's
biological clock is awry, so that going to bed and getting up are

out of kilter. Until some structured activity begins, one confronts infinite choices of what to do with "free" time. What do you do? How do you organize your time? You don't know anyone, the telephone (if there is one) does not ring, there are no meetings to attend, no assignments, no status to occupy, no network of which to be a part. All that seemed an onerous burden in the old place is missed desperately, and most humans move to "escape from freedom" by instituting routines.

The experience we have in mind here, though, is only one type of movement. It is the "move," where one does not travel for the fun of travel but, as did Zhivago, to get to a new place where one must, for a time, remain, and reorder one's life, perhaps in relation to the lives of others whom one must look after. It is the combination of responsibility and disorientation that engenders emotions like those felt by Zhivago when he finally reaches the Siberian estate.

In contrast to a move, from an old place to a new place, one may speak of travel, where one stays on the move. Travel, at least in romantic tradition, evokes emotions not of desolation but of freedom and excitement. A German song celebrates "wandering":

Der Mai ist gekommen, die Baume schlagen aus
Da bleibe der Lust hat, mit Sorgen zu Haus.

"May has come, the trees are blooming; let anyone who desires stay home with worries!" As for me, the singer resonates stirringly, I will go out, on the road, wandering, see beautiful mountains and valleys, do wondrous things and have marvelous adventures. Wandering beckons to us, too, in the form of hitchhiking and backpacking. Some remove the inconveniences and risks as well as the adventure of travel by taking organized tours. Others seek the greatest danger possible by rowing small boats across the ocean, flying tiny planes over the poles, and parachuting off skyscrapers.

Where does anthropological travel fit in all this? Popular media often depict it as adventurous; the anthropologist is Indiana Jones discovering the Lost Ark or the Temple of Doom. A real-life adventurer, Thor Heyerdahl, built a raft in prehistoric form, which he named *Kon-Tiki*, and sailed from Peru to Tahiti. His ostensible purpose was scientific, to prove that the ancient Peruvians could have done it and thereby influenced Pacific culture; whatever the scientific justification, sun-bronzed Nordics were permitted to carry out a manly adventure. One can read in the *National Geographic* of anthropologists who, in the same spirit, travel through jungle, desert, and mountains to live with lost tribes or discover lost cities. Or one can simply listen to what we term "field stories." Back from the field, luxuriating in "civilization," returnees tell of mishaps from finding a snake in one's sleeping bag to finding oneself in the midst of a revolution. I tell of my fieldwork in Indonesia, where within twenty-four hours a volcano erupted and my wife was bitten by a mad dog; of experiences in militant Muslim training camps; or, more calmly, of some mildly adventurous trip like this:

> By travelling "deck class" – which is to say, sleeping on the deck – you could go several thousand miles for ten dollars on an Indonesian ship. In 1970, as I was embarking on a study of the Indonesian Muslim movement, Muhammadijah, I had received permission from Muhammadijah to do a study of them, and they gave me a letter of introduction to all of their branches, which extended from northern Sumatra to Western New Guinea, some 3,000 miles of islands. I found out when a ship left, and went down to the dock in Jakarta, carrying my suitcase which was heavy with cameras and tape re-corders but lacking in certain essentials, as I was soon to realize. I joined a large mob of Indonesians who pushed through a large gate as soon as the guards opened it. We got on the boat deck, and I discovered that everyone else had brought a mat on which to sleep. Fortunately, in scrambling for a spot on the deck, I had become acquainted with a group of Indonesian students (from the agricultural college in Bogor on the way home to Sulawesi) and they let me share their mats. By now evening was coming and, as the ship cast off, supper was announced. The ten dollars included meals, too, for the two-week journey! But then it turned out that all meals came out of two vats in the hold, one containing rice and the other boiling water. Everybody lined up, and filled his bowl with rice and his cup with water. I had neither bowl nor cup. Again, a student came to the rescue. We shared his bowl and cup until, after several days at sea, we docked at Surabaya, and I bought a set for myself.

The trip had its adventurous aspect, but it was a slow way to get to where I was going to find out what I thought I needed to know.

What is the place of travel and adventure in the research of the anthropologist?

A sour opinion of adventure is given by anthropologist Claude Lévi-Strauss, himself author of the greatest anthropological travel-ogue, *Tristes Tropiques*. He begins, "Travel and travellers are two things I loathe and here I am, all set to tell the story of my adventures." He continues:

> Anthropology is a profession in which adventure plays no part; merely one of its bondages, it represents no more than a dead weight of weeks or months wasted en route; hours spent in idleness when one's informant had given one the slip; hunger, exhaustion, illness as like as not...[3]

Whatever Lévi-Strauss's professed cynicism, *Tristes Tropiques* is an enchanting if pessimistic evocation of wandering through jungles past abandoned railroad tracks and broken-down telephone wires in search of the pure primitive. The work is also autobiographical as the author reflects how he got into this strange occupation, inspired by a teacher whom he depicts as resembling a piece of vegetable matter. Travel and autobiography lead toward analysis, itself often ironic, of the cultural patterns of natives met in the jungle. As Lévi-Strauss travels and writes, he meditates philosophically and, in the end, adopts a posture of stoical detachment, professing himself happy simply to affirm his place in nature through an exchange of winks with a cat.

The ambivalent role of adventure in fieldwork is captured by a headline in the *Times Literary Supplement*: "Clerk not Gable." "Clerk" is pronounced in Britain as "Clark" is in America, so the headline is a pun announcing the contrast between a clerk and the swashbuckling adventurer of the type portrayed in old Hollywood films by Clark Gable. The article is, in fact, a review of a book that recounts an anthropologist's adventures, not all of them swashbuckling; but the point of the pun is that the adventurous aspect of fieldwork is often tempered by clerklike routines necessary to record information.[4]

Illustrative of the place of adventure in ordinary fieldwork is an account by Clifford Geertz, who tells of problems in gaining entry into Balinese society. He and his wife, Hildred, were treated courteously but as nonexistent: as having no place or being in the lives of the Balinese. Then the Geertzes attended a cockfight that, being illegal, was raided by the police. The Geertzes, like everyone else, fled. This incident made them the hit of the village. Everyone delighted in caricaturing their motions in running away, relishing details of their flight and embellishing memories of this misadventure that the anthropologists had shared with the natives. In this way the Geertzes acquired an identity in the community.[5]

Fieldwork

What is the difference between Geertz's account and the travels and tales of travel mentioned before? Geertz's account is certainly one of adventure, told with a certain literary zest, but it differs in result, and the telling has a different objective. The point of Geertz's tale is that this adventure (or misadventure) led to an essential if workaday step in fieldwork: to establish a role in the community. This step led to another: interpretation.

The three steps – experience, establishing an identity in the new setting, and interpretation – hint at the peculiar combination of subjectivity and objectivity, adventure and work, romanticism and pragmatism, that constitute so-called participant observation, which is at the core of anthropological fieldwork. Geertz's adventure is hardly what Lévi-Strauss claims: time wasted. But neither is it simply adventure for the hell of it; one is not just "on the road," one is "in the field," and one must move to find a place in it, then to understand it. For the adventurer, as for the tourist and other travelers, the places and people encountered are as nature: objects, passed by, looked at, perhaps photographed and noted, but that is all. The traveler perhaps undergoes hardships and even enters into poignant and romantic relationships as he moves toward his destination, but he is ever moving. The ethnographer comes to stay, for a while; for better or worse, he has to find a place. Is that different from the empathetic type of traveler who has a knack for hanging up his hat and staying – the seeker for truth who ends up meditating in an ashram in India or a monastery in Tibet for years, the mystic who, like Carlos Castaneda's Don Juan, finds his "spot"? There is a difference. The anthropologist cannot simply hang around or get absorbed. He must also record, describe, analyze, and, eventually, formulate, as best he can, the culture. Such a formulation is the result of fieldwork: the ethnography.

Fieldwork and the twice-born: a testimony
Travel for adventure has an external focus: coping with physical hardship, sensations of danger and strange places. Those travelers

who have gone farther physically, the astronauts, have not been notably articulate in describing the inner meaning of travel, and the physically perilous adventures – such as in mountain climbing – hinge on engineering more than poetry. Yet introspective tales of travel form an important genre in literature. The Germans have a term for it – the *Bildungsroman*, or "formative novel"; *Wilhelm Meisters Lehrjahre* (*William Master's Apprenticeship*) by Goethe is a famous example – a tale of an adolescent's adventures as he grows up. Such accounts unite movement from place to place with inner quest, search, and maturation through growing awareness and understanding. Travel is not only broadening but "deepening," or can be.

Fieldwork is a rite of passage, too. The field experience is said to be radically self-transforming; it is like psychoanalysis, like brainwashing, but it is also an initiation ritual that, through ordeals and insights, moves the initiate to a new level of maturity. A parallel is the conversion experience in which, to use a phrase popularized in fundamentalist Christianity, one is "born again." Like Saul on the road to Damascus, like Augustine or Martin Luther, the convert experiences a dramatic transformation; the scales fall from his eyes, he sees the world anew; in fact, he lives in a new world, for he is born again, a new person.

The analogy to conversion is perhaps too dramatic, but the fieldworker does undergo some kind of inner transformation. He experiences "culture shock" when he enters the field and a reverse shock when he comes home. During the work, he has eye-opening encounters, which shatter assumptions held all his life. Gradually he becomes, as we say, "acculturated," which means that he develops some degree of identity with the new culture and group, more often than not coming to think of them as "his people"; in some ways he experiences their lives more intensely than those of friends with whom he has grown up, in part because he is throwing his full being into learning to know them rather than dividing his energies among many pursuits, as in his normal life back home. If he persists in anthropology, he may spend the rest of his life setting forth insights based on this first experience of fieldwork. Such an account is like the testimony of the religious convert – a story of one's conversion experience. The language is different; the convert tells of himself, the anthropologist in his ethnography tells about the "natives," the others; but reporting the way "they are" often reveals much about the way "I am."

Given the formative power of the field experience, it is not surprising that the discipline hardly considers one an anthropologist, at least a sociocultural anthropologist, until one has had it. In this sense it is analogous to internship in medicine but perhaps even closer to combat in the military; the experience is partly training and certification but even more a rite of passage that ceremonially affirms one's fitness.

Such is the ideal. The actuality varies by circumstance, and anthropologists endlessly amuse each other, if not others, by sharing their own "war stories" about their field experiences. My own first fieldwork illustrates some elements of the rite of passage.

The purpose (as stated on the research proposal submitted to obtain funds to go to the field) was to learn how national values were communicated to ordinary people in Indonesia. To research this question, I went to Indonesia in September 1962, accompanied by my nonanthropologist wife. I stayed one year and exposed us to two things: first, eighty-two performances of a working-class Indonesian drama known as *ludruk*; second, the lives of those Indonesians in whose milieu *ludruk* had meaning. Contexts of "participant observation" ranged from the shantytown in which we lived to the back of the *ludruk* troupe's truck in which I once traveled. The year was not without adventure and hardship in the simple physical sense: lice, the steamy stench of the tropical slum, and such incidents as volcanic eruption and bites from a rabid dog (fortunately for us, no serious disease, which we were lucky to escape). A sense of disorientation is the main negative feeling I recall. In this "year of living dangerously," unstable economic and political conditions and unpredictable life situations were disturbing to us as well as to the Indonesians in a way difficult to convey to those who take for granted the remarkably stable systems of the West.

Balancing these situations was the tolerance and kindness of many, beginning with the remarkable mother in the Javanese family with whom we lived. These kindnesses are a poignant memory, marred by a guilt and regret that my rather relentless drive to collect and analyze data sometimes got in the way of human bonds.

The year, while apparently lacking a sharply dramatic "conversion," was intense. I have had jobs requiring manual labor, intellectual effort, and social sensitivity, but fieldwork required them all, and in an alien milieu. Our human relationships were sometimes deep and significant, but, in the Javanese fashion, they were also stylized and polite; yet, again, they were shot through with strain and sacrifice, on their part and ours. Some recount dramatic moments when the new culture grabbed and shook them, shattering their assumptions. My understandings grew more gradually.

The tangible results of the fieldwork were field notes (some six hundred pages, single-spaced, banged out on a cheap portable), tapes, photographs, articles, and books. This prosaic point reminds us that fieldwork is method as well as experience. It may have in it the potential of the rite of passage and the conversion experience, to transform the self and teach insight. But whatever its subjective aspect, it is also a method, even a scientific method, for attempting to characterize descriptively someone else's way of life.

Participation and observation
It was said of the poet Goethe that he deliberately had romantic affairs that he let run to the point where he could write about them but not be consumed by them (in fact, he finally took as his mate a woman of lower status than himself, as though to hold himself aloof from his companion). Something of this psychology would necessarily hold for the anthropologist, no matter how exuberantly gregarious his temperament may be. His task calls for both involvement and detachment, entry and exit. He must orchestrate his engagement so that his participation is also observation.

The lore is full of tales of anthropologists who went native: The young Oxford student Noone apparently married into the Ulu tribe of Malaysia and was never seen again by Westerners despite a long search by his brother. Kurt Onkel joined a tribe in Brazil and became Nimuendaju. Perhaps every fieldworker who has become absorbed in the life of a foreign group has felt a tug to go native. The reason is not only that most cultures have their attractions but also the nature of fieldwork. In modern society, most of us lead our lives narrowly – doing our jobs, carrying out our routines. We participate in group life actively and empathetically only part-time and after-hours, so to speak. In fieldwork, one endeavors to participate in the native group full-time. Although this can be enormously drain-

58

ing, it can also be exhilarating. Despite incomplete cultural understanding, one sometimes achieves a considerable depth of group participation. No wonder some go native! Yet the job of the anthropologist is, finally, not merely to experience or even join the group, but to analyze and understand it. To achieve that end, the participant must remain observer.

Fieldwork is hard enough in its practical aspects. Disease from bacteria and insects is almost inevitable, as is discomfort, whether from sleeping in strange places, eating strange foods, or simply living in poverty, and giving up familiar trappings to an extent few travelers imagine. There is danger, and some anthropologists have indeed been killed on the field site – though usually by accidents, and very rarely by the natives (contrary to the impression given by cartoons that show cannibals boiling visitors) – but on the whole anthropologists have been treated with a remarkable degree of kindness and tolerance. Bureaucratic obstacles – getting funds, visas, and permits, and simply getting there – are frustrating. Physical or political obstacles are sometimes extreme: One thinks of fieldwork accomplished among nomadic jungle groups, as among the Siriono and Penan; or in arctic environments, as among the Eskimos and Lapps; or in places at war, such as Iran, Algeria, or Vietnam; or among such groups as the Mafia and street gangs of Chicago and New York. Usually one must learn one or more new languages, some of which have complicated systems of sound and grammar radically different from our own and which may never have been studied or written down. Such practical obstacles impose limits, but at least they are external. What is killing about fieldwork is the combination of external and psychological demands. In a remote and physically trying situation, one must cope with problems of interpersonal communication and personal definition that few of us encounter in the comfortable environs of our own society. Most difficult, in fact irresolvable, is the dilemma of being at once participant and observer, of being both inside and outside, engaged and yet detached.

Fieldwork and related endeavors
Consider this list of activities; how does each compare to fieldwork?

Exploring
Excavating

History
Folklore
Literature
Journalism
Spying
Psychoanalysis
Social work
Missionary work
Administration
Childhood, friendship, and parenthood

All of these activities resemble fieldwork, but none has its distinctive combination of participation and observation. By comparing fieldwork to these activities – many of them familiar to us – we understand better the distinctive character of fieldwork.

Exploration, at first glance akin to fieldwork, does not require as much involvement in the local culture. In exploring, getting there is more than half the point, and staying there is rather beside the point. The great Western explorations, whether we think of Columbus's search for India, the British expeditions to the Nile, the voyage of the *Beagle*, Perry's trip to the Arctic, or the American and Russian explorations of space, have as their objective the discovery and exploration of a place where few, if any, Westerners have been before. Mobilization of much technology is required, hence large teams of people, ranging from native bearers to technicians to engineers and scientists. En route, the act of traveling itself is all-absorbing and rather takes priority over the recording of observation, although the ship's log and the diary (or the astronaut's occasional ongoing comments broadcast to television audiences) do have a place. Once at the destination, the team usually stays only briefly, and remains together as a team, perhaps keeping its ship or space ship as its home. Information is gathered in a rather detached manner, with the recording of customs – if any – being parallel to the recording of data on geology, flora, and fauna. (In fact, much of the early ethnological information was gathered by naturalists; Alfred Wallace, for example, not only shared with Charles Darwin in formulating the theory of evolution, but also reported many ethnographic as well as natural facts about Indonesia and Malaysia.) Parallel to collecting of geological, zoological, and botanical specimens is the collecting of ethnological specimens for display in museums. Sir Edward Tylor brought artifacts as well as knowledge back to Oxford, attested by a several-stories-high totem pole, bearing his name, at the Pitt-Rivers Museum there. Into the early twentieth century, the expedition remained the proper model for ethnological investigation. Nor is the tradition dead, for it is kept alive by the National Geographic Society in the United States and by explorers' clubs in both America and Britain.

Archaeological excavations share much with the exploration expedition. The *dig* requires the same mounting of elaborate technology by a team and the same detachment from the natives once one arrives at the site, because the primary interest is not in the living inhabitants but in their dead ancestors. (This detachment is not necessarily absolute, because in modern archaeological investigations of the so-called ethnohistorical type, the help and understanding of living natives are sought; but the objective remains the understanding of past lives rather than present ones.) Once digging, exploratory travel occurs in small compass beneath the surface of the earth, in this way differing from the expedition; but the psychology of the search is similar in that the seeker remains necessarily detached from the objects about which knowledge is sought. Conversation with these objects is not possible; the artifacts being excavated cannot speak except through technology: the trowel, the screen, the laboratory, and other tools of the archaeological trade. Although modern archaeology may strive mightily to understand the past culture reflected in artifacts, the archaeologist cannot – unless he has a time machine – participate directly in that culture.

History, sharing features of both ethnography and archaeology, resembles the latter in seeking its information from the dead: not from things, but from documents. Accordingly, the engagement of analyst with subject is necessarily restricted. An exception is the discipline called "oral history," where living people are interviewed in order to learn about their past. Even here, the sustained engagement in a community that is characteristic of ethnographic fieldwork is not typical; instead, the individual is interviewed outside the context of his contemporary community, and his oral utterance is transformed into a written document, through the technology of the recorder and the typewriter.

Folklore resembles oral history, indeed, was a model for it, but has traditionally entailed greater involvement by the folklorist in the culture whose lore he desires to record and understand; one thinks of the great collectors, such as Oxford's Cecil Sharp, living and traveling in Appalachia in a time when conditions were primitive. Still, "collecting" is the key concept. Traditionally, folklorists have striven to collect, to record and reproduce, discrete forms: ballads, tall tales, crafts or – to take contemporary examples – blues, toasts, and house designs.[6] Engagement in the community is secondary to this primary task of recording the forms produced by the individual: the singer, the teller of tales, the player of dulcimer or banjo, or other folk creators.

The writing of journalism and literature is difficult to characterize, for these are less academic disciplines than ways of perceiving and telling about whatever is deemed worth seeing and hearing. Still, certain tendencies can be noted. Standard front-page journalism is aimed at "getting the news." As humorously depicted in Evelyn Waugh's *Scoop*, that endeavor may locate the journalist in exotic places, but he does not usually find it necessary or even possible to become deeply part of the local community; normally, he moves in, gets his story, and moves out. The story is restricted to a specific chain of events, such as the palace coup as pieced together from observation and interview, or some notable opinion, as recorded in a single interview with some notable person.

Literature and journalism transformed into literature delve deeply into the character of culture and community and the experience of individuals, but are certainly not confined to the external pattern of an event. Nonfictional literary journalism may entail remarkable engagement and descriptive power, as in Truman Capote's *In Cold Blood*, which reconstructs the milieu and world of Kansas killers. Much can be learned from fiction writers concerning exotic places, as from Lawrence Durrell on the Near East, Anthony Burgess on Malaya, and García Márquez on tropical America. But the literary writer usually works somewhat differently from the ethnographer. Like the ethnographer, he may become deeply engaged, but typically without the constraint to collect information systematically; thus, he may become involved with a certain person or a certain family, from which he desires a distinctive experience, which becomes the germ of his plot. The ethnographer is normally compelled to participate in a fairly balanced fashion in a range of situations in order to present a holistic picture of the community and its culture or of some facet of it. Rarely does one take the view of a single character, group, or experience, because the task entails treating the total configuration. Western literary works usually present the exotic culture as a backdrop for some Western character or small group of characters; think of the writings of Somerset Maugham or Joseph Conrad, or, for that matter, Durrell or Burgess. Despite the similarities of their tasks, the difference is clear. Almost no one has managed to write both superlative literature and superlative ethnography.

What about the spy? The ethnographer is often suspected of being one, especially in this day of spying; in fact, there are cases where intelligence agents have posed as ethnographers, and cases where ethnographers have been hired by intelligence agencies. Ethnographers who find themselves living in a home boasting a collection of weapons of the IRA, having as neighbors members of the Viet Cong or as informants members of the Mafia, can hardly avoid learning of activities regarded as illegal by some authorities, or of interest to some country or other. And in some situations, ethnographers necessarily must move in suspect circles in order to get their work done, or simply to survive: If nothing else, they, like the natives, may be forced to patronize the black market or some other illicit trade. But if they are to uphold the ethics of ethnography, ethnographers could hardly differ more from spies. The essence of spies is that they pose as what they are not, in order to learn secrets. Anthropologists must declare their objectives openly to those with whom they are engaged in participant observation, must explain as best they can who they are and what they are about, and should not trick or force informants to divulge what they do not wish to divulge. Everyone knows instances when ethnographers did not fully conform to this recipe, and some situations render it difficult to do so entirely, but the principles are clear. Spying is a manipulative activity, ethnography a sharing one, at least in principle.

Spying, which has an explicitly manipulative and negative objective, bears one resemblance to psychoanalysis: Both draw information from individuals that they consciously wish to withhold. Unlike spying, this manipulation serves, in psychoanalysis, an ostensibly positive end, namely, a cure. Some ethnographers have actually been professional psychoanalysts, and others have employed the techniques of the psychoanalytical interview as part of fieldwork. An example is Geza Roheim, a disciple of Freud's, who did this among Australian Aborigines. The two disciplines have been combined, as in George Devereux's psychoanalysis of a Plains Indian.[7] Although resembling the ethnographer in trying to delve deep within the psyche so as to uncover implicit patterns of behavior, the psychoanalyst uses a different technique. For one thing, in the classical and common arrangement, the physician does not go out into the field; the patient comes to him, in his office or clinic. Although the analyst, through "transference" and other relationships, may become deeply and even passionately involved with individual patients, he does not — as analyst — cast himself into a community; he remains in the role of physician, and many institutional bulwarks save him from risking his identity by being absorbed into an alien group. Further, the patient is motivated to talk to the analyst by his desire for cure, whereas the native informant may have no such specific motive in talking with the anthropologist, even if, in fact, a kind of insight and objectivity may be gained through the opportunity to talk about one's own culture. Because the psychoanalyst is a curer, his relation to the patient is not as seeker of the patient's knowledge so much as one who tries to change him; the ethnographer is placed in the position of the learner, the student of what is to be taught by the culture.

The social worker and the missionary resemble the physician in that they are out to do good, to give aid, perhaps ultimately religious salvation. Social workers are normally more confined to their offices. Missionaries move into the midst of the field for longer periods and with more complete commitment of self than any other people of the types we have considered; in fact, much of the best ethnography has been done by missionaries. Still, social workers, missionaries, and others hold to a purpose not merely of learning from the natives but of changing and transforming them. So long as this objective is held, one is necessarily forced to restrict one's openness to learning from the native; but a scientific objective narrows perception also, and the detachment of the missionary is probably less than that of the "objective" scientist.

Administrators, like physicians, social workers, and others, have a practical end toward which they organize their relations with the local culture. Like missionaries, colonial administrators in fact sometimes became extremely knowledgeable of the local setting and reported valuable information; on the whole, this is less often true of modern foreign-service administrators, who are usually stationed in a place for a shorter time and with more elaborate barriers of bureaucracy between themselves and the locals. (One thinks, for example, of the embassy officials in many of the world's capitals. Many do not speak the local language, and they travel in chauffered limousines, live in foreign luxury neighborhoods, send their children to special schools, eat food shipped in from their home countries, and are buffered from local contact by their servants and clerks.) Whatever the specific situation, however, administrators are necessarily governed in their relations by the tasks they must fulfill and, therefore, must restrict their local involvement.

At the far extreme from detachment are the roles of child, friend, and parent. All three roles, or something like them, will be played by the ethnographer. He enters the field as a child, ignorant of the new culture or situation, and he must learn painfully the native language and way of life. At the same time, he is sometimes treated as a parent, for he is usually from a wealthier society than those among whom he works (what has been termed "studying up" – fieldwork among the elite – is rare in anthropological fieldwork). Perhaps owing to egalitarian biases drawn from Western and especially American culture, the aim of many fieldworkers is to become something like a friend. The fieldworker would like to be treated as an equal, a peer, accepted as competent in the language and culture rather than regarded as either a powerful outsider or a foolish burden. Simply in physical terms, that may tax his resources; one thinks, for example, of one hardy ethnographer who skied fifty miles a day at subzero temperatures while working as a Lapp herder for four years and at the same time learning the culture, or of those who try to keep up with Andean Indians whose lives have been spent at high altitudes. The social difficulties are yet more complex; perhaps these can be illustrated, in part, by a dream that, I think, reflects some of the conflicting forces and engagements of fieldwork.

In this dream, I encountered on the street a beggar from the Third World; of indeterminate ethnicity, he could have been a Mexican or an Indonesian. I decided to put some money in his tin cup, but had no coins; I therefore placed a bill there, then tried to take some change from the cup. In doing so, I mixed my money with the beggar's, and we could not straighten out whose was whose. Finally, we gave up trying to solve the problem, and by this time were engaged in a conversation. He revealed that he had great fear of losing his money and wanted to exchange it for American Express traveler's checks! I pointed out that he was sitting in front of a bank, and suggested that he go in and buy the checks. He demurred, saying they would not accept a beggar in such a place, and asked if I would buy them. I agreed, and did so, but now all of his money was in my power, for only if I signed the checks could his money be used. We discussed this problem, and he divulged that he had always desired to travel, so he suggested that we go together on a trip. Inextricably entangled, I woke up.

Whatever may have been the personal meanings in this dream, they express the kinds of dilemmas of social relationship that field-workers encounter. However much they may desire to be simply objective seekers of knowledge who share in this quest with the natives on an egalitarian basis, they become entwined in relations of power and participation; in the dream, I began by trying to help and ended by entanglement, the end of which was not revealed.

The techniques of encounter with other cultures and situations that have been cataloged above all boast arrangements to shield the person from engagement; this is true of expeditions, digs, and the practical activities, as well as, in a different sense, journalism and literature, history and folklore. Ethnographers wear their own armor, but it is perhaps flimsier.

Whatever the balance of engagement and distance that constitutes their ethnographic experience, the proof is in the pudding. Ethnographers must finally record those understandings gained and then somehow communicate them. Nothing is less useful (unless it be meaningless facts and figures) than vague memories sloppily logged and never reported. It is not enough, just to come home.

Interpretation

Description and interpretation

One may distinguish two aspects of ethnographic research: the data and their meaning. Data are the acts or objects that the ethnographer perceives and describes. Examples might be a vase or a house, a rite or an utterance, an exchange of goods or of pleasantries. Such objects and acts are perceived by the senses; they are seen, heard, smelled, touched.

These elements are parts of wider wholes. The wholes include the setting and consciousness of both the actors and the observer. How does the ethnographer decide that a lump of clay is a "vase" or that the act of someone handing an object to someone else and receiving something in return is an "exchange"? The ethnographer categorizes and labels these acts and objects, and this categorizing and labeling reflects his own situation and consciousness as well as that of the actors. Description is also interpretation, for one categorizes and labels – indeed, constructs – his data even as he "records" them.

Ethnographic research is sometimes termed, too simply, as "collecting data." Why is this too simple? Because the ethnographer does not simply gather facts, as a botanist might gather plants or an archaeologist potsherds. The ethnographer's mind is not a bucket or basket, but a searchlight. One seeks and highlights, notices this but not that. One abstracts and constructs "facts" from the flow of experience.

Anthropologist Rodney Needham tells this story:

> The story has been told (I do not remember the source) that Picasso was once reproached for distorting human features out of recognition. A portrait, his critic contended, ought to look like the person portrayed. Picasso demurred, and suggested that it was not quite so straightforward a business as that; the idea of looking just like something was a bit more difficult than the interlocutor supposed. The critic thereupon produced a photograph from his wallet, showed it to Picasso, and said: "There, you see, that's my wife, and that's what she looks like." Picasso looked carefully at the little print and asked, with a hint of surprise, "Just like that?" Confidently the critic confirmed that she looked exactly like that. "Hmm," said Picasso, "isn't she rather small?"[8]

A pianist played a piece. "What does it mean?" a critic asked. The pianist responded by simply playing the piece again. The artist and the musician make the same point: an aesthetic form is already interpretation. The point holds for science, inasmuch as a scientific description is an aesthetic form.

The impossibility of making a carbon copy of reality and therefore the necessity of interpreting even as one describes is true in all sciences. One definition of fact captures this point: A fact is a percept viewed through a frame of reference. The observer-describer brings to his object of observation his own theories and questions as well as implicit biases and attitudes, and these set a framework for his perceptions.

Among the sciences, the ethnographer has a special situation. His study is of, and therefore among, humans. Owing to our laboratory image of the physical scientist, we think of him as cold and detached, uninvolved with that which he manipulates through his experiments. This stereotype is false even in physical science, but it is true that the physical scientist differs from his objects of study in a way the social scientist does not. "It takes one to know one" makes sense in describing the study of humans but not in describing the study of rocks and acids. In ethnography, detachment is impossible to sustain. The ethnographer is necessarily involved – to varying degrees – in the human encounter that is fieldwork. Rather than standing aloof, observing and recording in a detached way, the ethnographer distills his ethnography from his own experience in the flow of native life. One may even say that the ethnographer and the natives work together to construct the data and interpretation that we call ethnography.

In fact, in fieldwork the encounter and interpretation occur on both sides. Here is a paraphrase of some comments made by an "informant" to fieldworkers about other fieldworkers. The remarks, addressed to a colleague and me about two other colleagues (whom we shall call Dick and Jane), were made by a Primitive Baptist elder (let's call him Jones) from Appalachia, where all four of us were doing research. The elder begins by saying, "I lost Jane at Union [the name of a church where Jane was hearing him preach] on women being a type [symbol] in the church [the topic of his sermon]. Well, she called me one day, had her little tablet [to take notes]. I got her!" Elder Jones goes on to recount his discussion with Jane, where he proved to her by Scripture that the major symbol or "type" of the church is womankind. He then shifts the subject to Dick. He tells of sensing early that Dick would marry Jane (which he eventually did). Then he tells of writing Dick a letter congratulating him. He gleefully recounts reminding Dick of his (Jones's) early intuition and that he (Dick) once remarked "You're a close observer, Elder Jones." Torn out of context, this conversation doubtless makes little sense to the reader, but it does illustrate how the "native" alertly observes the ethnographer, as well as vice versa – a dialogue only one side of which ethnographers usually are privileged to hear.

Fieldwork is not, of course, merely encounter. It also entails systematic procedures. One must often learn one or more languages, must map the layout of the community, complete a census of its inhabitants, and plot their genealogical interrelationships. Depending on their project's focus, the ethnographers may measure acreage, crop output, and the calories the people consume. They may administer psychological tests or carry out physiological measurements. Certainly they will record great masses of notes on whatever they observe, and they may even computerize or otherwise systematize such data. And of course, as the quotation opening this chapter reminds us, they must ask questions. But the human encounter, and the sense one can make of it, remains the central ethnographic experience.

Positivism and interpretation

"Logical Positivism" is the name of a school of philosophy originating in Vienna early in this century, but more broadly it is a kind of thinking that pervades Western culture, especially the sciences. Put simply, positivism postulates that there exists a body of facts "out there," in the "real world," independent of our perception and interpretation. All scientific knowledge must be grounded in these facts, and the farther we get from them, the less is our knowledge to be trusted; theory and speculation are suspect. We can, however, formulate hypotheses that must be checked against the facts through rigorous, systematic procedures. Correctly followed, such procedures lead us to reject false hypotheses.

Positivism itself has evolved during this century, but opposing viewpoints have also emerged. One view, which can be termed "interpretive," is that no facts exist independent of perceivers; the definition given earlier – that a fact is a percept viewed through a frame of reference – would fit this position, for "fact" is seen as a construction reflecting both the perspective of perceivers and the world that they perceive. If this is so, then the systematic procedures favored by the positivists are not as objective as they assume, for when one moves from theory to hypothesis to fact, one does not escape theory, because it is entailed by how one construes the facts themselves. Fact, as well as theory, is interpretation.

Now, within anthropology and the social sciences are found both the positivist and the interpretive viewpoints, with myriad shadings and colorings of each. Simplifying, however, we can identify the dominant viewpoint in the social sciences – psychology, sociology, economics – as positivist and an influential viewpoint in ethnography as interpretive. A somewhat overstated contrast between the positivist social scientist and the interpretive ethnographer serves to highlight the distinctive logic of each.

The positivist social scientist begins with a hypothesis. To test that hypothesis, he carries out a systematic investigation, through a survey, an experiment, or the like. This research generates data. By means of these data, the hypothesis is disconfirmed or tentatively confirmed.

The ethnographer may also follow such a procedure to a degree, but the unanticipated realities of fieldwork often jar it loose. One may enter the field with a specific question or hypothesis, but in the field one encounters something challenging the very formulation of that question; one realizes that the question is misleading or irrelevant, then one's attention turns to the encounter itself and one tries to make sense of it. In short, research in fieldwork often begins with encounter, then proceeds to interpretation.

The positivist model may seem to differ from the ethnographic only in that it moves from idea to data instead of from data to idea. More emphatically, it may seem that the positivist model is more rational, that it is based on planning, whereas the other is chaotic: Jump in. Sink or swim. Fly by the seat of your pants. The differences run deeper.

The positivist model is rational, but it is rationality as defined by the observer rather than by the actor. Having defined your hypothesis, rationality and efficiency dictate that you limit your test to only those data that are relevant. Accordingly, you create these data, manufacture them through your procedure. In psychology, this procedure is typically the experiment; in sociology, the survey questionnaire; in economics, various kinds of statistical measurement.

The term "manufacture" is appropriate because the items collected tend to be standardized, as in mass production. In the experiment, you run each trial repeatedly, and in a survey you ask the same question repeatedly so that you can amass a large amount of data. In each instance, you control the stimulus and thus standardize the subject's response. When you have recorded many responses to each kind of stimulus, you can begin to analyze statistically the relationship between stimulus and response, and other kinds of pattern.

The ethnographer comes closer than the experimenter or the opinion pollster to encountering the data as it is made by the native – in his daily behavior and conversation, his rituals and work, his conflicts and struggles. Two qualifications to this picture must be made, however, lest one accept the image of the ethnographer as a passive, amorphous sponge, soaking up the particularities of the exotic experience, in comparison to another stereotype: the authoritarian psychologist or sociologist forcing his categories on the subject. The first qualification is that the ethnographer does affect his encounter with the other; he is actively engaged in constructing his data. In his own way, he is an experimenter too. The second qualification, which tempers the first, is that the natives themselves tend to standardize their acts, utterances, and things. Their rituals and ceremonies, their tales and songs, and other expressive and sacred forms have great coercive power that override external influences, ethnographer included. Would the actors change a rite to suit a lone ethnographer, when they must also please the gods, not to mention a large congregation? Accordingly, the experiment or survey questionnaire standardizes data to suit standards of the observer; expressive forms standardize data to suit standards of the actor. The ethnographer can take advantage of the natives' standardization through paying attention to their own summaries of their meanings and through noting commonalities that their own forms display. It is not happenstance that ethnographers record verbatim rituals and ceremonies, tales and songs, and native philosophical arguments. This is not idle collecting of old lore, but ethnographic analysis that is quite structured and precise – after listening carefully to the native's own way of being structured and precise.

Data manufactured by the native are generally thicker or richer than those manufactured by the observer. This stands to reason, and not just because the native knows more about his life than does the observer; it stems also from difference in purpose. The purpose of the survey or experiment is to simplify, to exclude extraneous influences or "variables." The ideal experiment would control all variables but the one to be investigated. If a question is ambiguous, you do not know what the response means. If an experiment is muddled, you do not know which variables cause the effect. For certain purposes, then, data should be "thin," that is, should pertain only to the variable under investigation. Native expression is not thin. It is manufactured not to answer some restricted question or test some narrow hypothesis but to express the native's being. Ceremonies and rituals, myths and legends – all are "thick" with meanings; they distill into form a plethora of values, ideas, and experiences. Encounter with such forms is inevitably confusing, but the confusing richness of meaning leads to deeper understanding, provided we sort out the patterns and principles behind the meaning. This effort is what we call interpretation.

At another level, too, ethnographic data are "thick." Such data must be abstracted from complex human relationships, those that earlier we have termed "multiplex." These are thick and complexly intertwined, in contrast to "thin" or "uniplex" relations that ramify into only a restricted part of our lives. Consider the contrast, noted earlier, between one's relation to a clerk or technician whom one did not know in any other capacity, as opposed to one's relationship to a parent or spouse, or to an intimate friend or a fellow believer in a communal sect. Ethnographers tend to become involved with these thick relationships, and this emphasis carries implications for their method.

For the experimenter or the survey analyst, sampling is a key technique. To sample is to select a large number of equal but independent units. Say that a surveyer asks a sample of three hundred persons if they will vote Democratic or Republican. He then generalizes from this sample of three hundred to the total population of the town, country, state, or nation. This is the way polling is done, as in predictions of election results. Now, if you want to generalize from a sample to a population, you want the sample to be representative of the population. You would not ask three hundred members of a single family, or a single church, then generalize from them to a diversified population. You would fear that the responses of one member of a group may affect those of the others, or that they all share some feature not characteristic of the larger population, such as being of the Smith family or of the Methodist or Catholic church. Instead, you would try to sample randomly, which does not mean wildly; it means that you systematically select in a way not determined by the question you wish to ask (for example, you would not sample only among the rich or only among the poor in order to predict whether the nation will vote Republican or Democrat). In short, the survey analyst would avoid precisely those relationships which the ethnographer prizes.

The reason for this difference is that the survey analyst wants to avoid confusing factors such as multiplex relationships, whereas the ethnographer seeks these because cross-cutting resonances, reinforcements, and clues that come from working intensively in a thickly interrelated group enrich his understanding of particular meaning. In the end, the ethnographer may not be sure how representative of the larger population his group of intensive study is, but he will have a deeper knowledge of meanings in that group. Is this simply learning "a lot about a little" versus "a little about a lot"? It is not only that. Not only the scope but the quality of the ethnographic research is distinctive; active involvement in a small group means that the group *teaches* the investigator, and this kind of learning differs from analysis of responses viewed in a detached way.

Owing to the richness of learning acquired through the ethnographic method, it is sometimes touted as an excellent way to discover meanings and gain insights. It is also doubted as a way of verifying (or refuting) theories, because it samples only a small segment of a population. A swallow does not make a summer, and detailed analysis of a small group does not prove a universal principle. A detailed study can, however, forcefully call into question claims of universal theory and can creatively suggest insights to enrich such theory. This is one way ethnographic interpretation contributes to the study of human affairs.

An example of interpretation: the construction of substance
Following is a conversation recently overheard. The setting: the waiting room of a physician. The cast: X, a very old white man, an eminent citizen of this town; Y, a middle-aged black woman, employed as a maid for a younger acquaintance of X; Z, a youngish

white woman, who knows both X and Y. Let us call X "Mr. Hargrove," Y "Bessie," and Z "Jane."

Jane and Mr. Hargrove are seated when Bessie enters. Jane greets Bessie: "Hello, Bessie. Bessie, you remember Mr. Hargrove?" Bessie replies, "Yes, I do," then addresses Hargrove: "You doin' okay?" Hargrove: "I'm old enough to say, 'Very well, thank you.' "

How might one interpret Mr. Hargrove's reply? Why did he not simply reply, "Fine, how are you?" or "Sure, you okay?" or something of the sort? I was puzzled but hardly felt it appropriate to jump up and ask him what he meant; in any case, immediately after uttering his cryptic comment he was wheeled off to the doctor. The setting is a familiar one, and the language is English, but the challenge resembles that facing the ethnographer a thousand times a day in exotic settings as he overhears strange languages: how to interpret what he hears and observes? We can never know exactly what Hargrove meant, but the exercise of interpreting can serve to make concrete some of what is explained abstractly about the process of interpretation.

In a situation like this, it is helpful to begin with patterns that are fairly clear and that form a context for the action or utterance to be interpreted. Distinctions of age and possibly of gender, ethnicity, and social class frame this situation. Bessie and Jane are female, Hargrove male. Jane and Hargrove are white, Bessie is black. Hargrove is an eminent man in the town, Jane is apparently of his social class, and Bessie is employed as a servant by someone in his class. Hargrove is old – almost ninety – while Bessie is in her sixties and Jane her late thirties. The distinctions of age, ethnicity, and class are all reflected in Jane's using the first name (possibly nickname) of the middle-aged black woman and the last name of the elderly white man. But what is one to make of Hargrove's answer to Bessie? Whatever he may mean, the formality of his words contrasts with the informality of hers. Furthermore, he associates his formal style with his advanced age: "I'm old enough to say, 'Very well, thank you.' " Is his crotchety implication that, if he is old enough to answer in that formal manner, then he is also old enough to be addressed in an equally formal manner ("Are you doing well?") instead of with the breezy "You doin' okay?" If this interpretation is correct, Hargrove is affirming a certain traditionalism, a value of respect for the elderly in the face of conflicting values of informal congeniality. And if this is true, he is affirming values that have deep roots. He taps traditions of honor and respect as well as perhaps a genteel racism and chauvinism in the southern regional culture of which Hargrove and this town are part. Beyond that, he affirms broadly human values concerning the relations between young and old, male and female, and the significance of manners, language, and ritual in civilized conduct. The Javanese would find his attitude perfectly understandable!

One should not make too much of this thin slice of life, but one can learn from it. Here, in a physician's waiting room during a brief and cryptic exchange, premises of culture are affirmed, affronted, reaffirmed – in a word, negotiated. Culture is being constructed, right here, on the spot, before our eyes. At the same time, the ethnographer is doing his own constructing as he records the conversation and context (omitting a thousand times more than he records) while struggling to make sense of it. He is interpreting.

Resembling fieldwork in some respects, in one the example differs. Here the ethnographer is the silent observer. He does not enter the conversation. Such detachment is permitted in the waiting room, one of those peculiar modern arrangements that permits such bureaucratized alienation, but this situation is not typical in anthropological fieldwork. Imagine that events unfold as in a play. Say that a blizzard forces everyone to remain in the waiting room overnight. In that forced intimacy (so many experiences of which any fieldworker can recall painfully), the anthropologist would presumably enter the conversation with Hargrove, Jane, and Bessie. The situation would begin to resemble fieldwork, for the anthropologist would be engaged – he would be a participant observer rather than merely an observer, and the contact would become an encounter. Now meanings would be negotiated not only by the actors but also by the anthropologist, who would become, in that divided sense peculiar to his profession, himself an actor-spectator.

Notice how this formulation affects our understanding of the nature of culture. Hargrove, Jane, and Bessie are constructing culture. At the same time, the ethnographer, through interpretation, is formulating a pattern of culture to make sense of the conversation. Culture is not a fixed thing but a negotiated formulation, a working definition that serves the moment and the circumstance, for both actor and ethnographer. Substance is no longer separate from method, for the construction of culture is part of the fieldwork itself.

At least, this is the way contemporary ethnography tends to see it. There was a time, going back to Sir Edward Tylor, when anthropology did tend to regard culture as a thing, a static object. Culture was a collection of customs, embodied in physical artifacts brought home and exhibited in museums. Culture was also mental artifacts – beliefs, values, norms – that remained relatively constant and were transmitted from generation to generation intact, unless disrupted by some outside force.

Such a view is what many anthropologists regard as the old one, now modified by a stronger sense of dynamism. In the new perspective, culture is seen more as in our illustration, as a construction incessantly negotiated by the actors and interpreted by the anthropologist. The actors in any situation – whether it be a five-minute exchange or a society enduring for centuries – are engaged in a struggle to impose cultural and social meaning on the chaos of existence. This struggle is motivated not only by the quest for meaning but also by political, economic, and natural forces, and culture is sought rather than simply given. This is especially the case, of course, in the unstable Third World situations where anthropologists have increasingly found themselves since the end of World War II, but the pattern is visible even in the antiseptic, cozy setting of a local physician's waiting room.

Generalization
Particularizing and generalizing at the extremes – these are the dual features of anthropology when compared to the other social sciences, humanities, and the natural sciences.

At one extreme, fieldwork leads to involvement with a particular group and to learning about that group. The ethnographer identifies with that group, which becomes "my village," "my tribe," or "my people." He then becomes a notorious nay-sayer. To every generalization that is posed about human conduct, he is tempted to say, "My people don't do it that way." (As the Indonesian proverb has it, "Lain desa, lain adat" ["another village, another custom"]; particularism blocks generalization.) Then, having experienced a kind of conversion to a certain way of life during fieldwork, the ethnographer may resemble the evangelist who spends his career preaching the truths of that experience; everything that he has to say about humanity is couched in terms of this early experience. On the other hand, the ethnographer may become so steeped in the language and life of his village or tribe that his descriptions of them are intelligible to no one except himself and them.

At the other extreme, anthropology aspires to global generalization. Philosophers may discern truths of human nature by searching their souls; psychologists, by testing and experimenting with American college students; but the anthropologist claims to generalize from a wider base: the cultures of the world, not restricted to the American, the Western, the civilized, but including peoples from every place and way of life.

Of this ambitious project, E. E. Evans-Pritchard is reported to have remarked, shrewdly, "There's only one method in social anthropology – the comparative method – and that is impossible."[9] Evans-Pritchard implies two truths. No ethnographic description is entirely particularistic, all are comparative in at least one sense: the ethnographer must communicate the truths of the culture he studies to members of another culture, that of his readers; such communication entails implicit comparison. The second truth is that comparison is impossible because nothing is comparable. Each society and each culture, like each snowflake and each fingerprint, is unique – incomparable. The classic experiment that is the ideal in natural science is not, therefore, feasible in anthropology. In the classic experiment, all factors but one are controlled. If you want to ascertain whether smoking causes cancer, the ideal method is to compare two groups that are alike in every way except that one is of smokers and the other is not, then see which has more cancer. Unfortunately, it is never possible to find groups that are alike in every way except one; you may match age, sex, income, and so on, but there will always be differences. This difficulty is exacerbated when comparing societies or cultures because each is so complicated. One might compare, say, China and Japan and conclude that Japan's form of government explains its more rapid industrialization. But China and Japan differ in many other respects, too, so that one cannot easily isolate a single cause. Nevertheless, the comparison can be instructive. Doing it, one learns something about each culture that one would not by examining it alone, and one gains new insight into various kinds of relationships. On a wider scale, comparison can even permit tentative generalization about humanity: How else to find what everybody has in common than to inquire about everybody?

The comparative method aims at essentially two goals: to show how humans are alike and to show how they differ, and why.

Universals

Based on surveying the peoples of the world, anthropologists have occasionally claimed that certain patterns are universal. It has been said, for example, that all human groups boast some form of religion, of art, and of family life (whereas such institutions as government and schools are not universal). Others have claimed that all humans wage war, or at least have aggressive inclinations (a claim contested by those who find war a response to particular conditions). Another favorite claim is that all human groups have incest taboo: a prohibition against marriage among certain classes of relatives. This last claim is instructive in pointing to the kinds of qualifications one must introduce when hazarding generalizations about humankind. The incest taboo, for example, varies in terms of which classes of relatives are prohibited mates. Mating and marriage between parents and children and among siblings are prohibited widely, but mating among close cousins is not only permitted but preferred or prescribed in certain societies and prohibited in others. Among the royalty and elite, for example, marriage of cousins is common, but the most interesting custom for anthropologists is that known as "matrilateral cross-cousin marriage." Many tribal societies throughout the world prescribe or prefer that the male marry the daughter of his mother's brother. Yet these same societies forbid the marriage of cousins who are biologically just as close, that is, parallel cousins where the linking relative is the same sex as the parent, as in father's brother's son and mother's sister's daughter. The reasons for this custom are too complex to cite here; the point is that, although the incest taboo may be universal or widespread, the specific prohibition varies. In some societies, the incest taboo is suspended under special circumstances. Among the ancient Egyptians and the Hawaiians, for example, marriage of brothers to sisters was permitted among the royalty, apparently on the ground that only royalty were good enough for royalty. Too, the gods of mythology are often permitted incest, apparently owing to a similar principle. In short, anthropologists can define the incest taboo as a human universal but only by careful definition.

Universal human tendencies appear in thought as well as conduct. As noted in Chapter 1, the structuralists postulate that all humans think similarly, for example, that humans think dualistically. According to structuralist research, human cultures everywhere classify the world into such oppositional categories as male and female, spiritual and temporal, and right and left. If such patterns of thought are indeed universal, why might that be? Some would suggest that the structure of the human brain, with its left and right hemispheres, is responsible for generating this dualism and other panhuman patterns of thought. Whatever the answer, one implication is clear. In contrast to the kind of explanation of human behavior favored by most philosophers and social scientists of the modern Anglo-American tradition, structuralism would favor another viewpoint. The Anglo-American tradition, known as empiricism, has argued that humans are so plastic that their ways of thinking and acting are explicable primarily as responses to their environment. Structuralism follows a philosophy known as rationalism, which postulates that the human mind has innate categories, which surface regardless of the environment. Structuralism, then, is disposed to discover universal human qualities.[10]

Covariation

Comparative studies seek not only commonalities but differences, then inquire how one difference is associated with another. As in the search for universals, one may divide these studies into those focusing on conduct and those focusing on thought. One may also distinguish between typologies, laws, and mathematical formulations.

Typologies simply recognize and define clusters of traits; that is, as one surveys the societies of the world, one sees that where trait X is found, so also is trait Y, and where A is found, so also is B. A cluster of covarying traits is a "type." A crude but long-standing and rather useful typology is based on mode of subsistence: hunting and gathering, herding, farming, industry, for example. Social and cultural traits are then noted when they commonly occur in association with one or the other of these modes of subsistence. For example, centralized state bureaucracy is found primarily in food-growing or industrial societies, not in those relying solely on hunting and gathering. Hunting and gathering societies are usually organized as small family bands. Large unilineal-descent groups – clans or lineages – flourish in agrarian societies, not in either of the extremes of subsistence: hunting and gathering or industrial. This kind of typology is often organized as an evolutionary sequence, in which the less exploitive technologies and their associated sociocultural arrangements evolve toward more exploitive societies. Such an evolutionary scheme was emphasized by the nineteenth-century founders of anthropology, and in somewhat revised form it continues to be of use in present-day anthropological theory.

Whereas typologies suggest covariations and regularities, laws state those covariations explicitly. In an evolutionary scheme like that just mentioned, for example, one can see general trends such as the movement from simple to complex (in the specific sense of social organization, for example, where hunting and gathering societies tend to be egalitarian, whereas agrarian and industrial societies differentiate into classes). Such a trend can be stated as a kind of law, to the effect, say, that an increase in energy use increases social complexity. Anthropologists have been leery of formulating such laws, because exceptions seem always to crop up (as Montesquieu, Kant, and others have suggested, humans follow natural laws in their physical aspect, but seem to transcend law in their cultural aspect). However, some have hazarded them. An example is Service's law of evolutionary potential. This so-called law holds that breakthroughs in cultural evolution are more likely to occur at the periphery than at the center of a civilization. History is a relay race: A central group carries the baton of civilization to a certain point, then hands it to a peripheral group that becomes, for a time, central. The last become first, then the first last, as history proceeds in a geographical zigzag.[11]

The relationships postulated by these evolutionary typologies and laws are based on a functionalist or causal kind of analysis, such that A covaries with B because A is functionally or causally related to B: Agriculture is found with states because it sets necessary conditions, without which the state could not function. The condition of being at the periphery sets the stage for cultural advances that then catapult periphery into center. The inspiration for this kind of causal-functional generalization is the positivistic model of natural sciences.

Another kind of generalization pertains less to human conduct than to human thought and is inspired more by mathematics and logic than by the natural sciences. This is the sort of generalization favored by the structuralists, in contrast to that favored by the evolutionists. The structuralist may, without asserting causal connections or functional interrelationships, summarize the vast scope of ethnographic fact as a small number of rules or mathematical formulae. Needham, for example, defined seven principles designed to summarize all the varieties of kinship systems.[12] Leach constructed formulas that stated the logical (and empirical) implications of certain kinds of sociological patterns for certain kinds of ideological patterns.[13] In the most ambitious proposal of all, but one not actually carried out, Lévi-Strauss suggested that we construct a chart, analogous to the periodic chart in chemistry, which would define all the basic components that make up human culture, such that any given culture (whether actually existing or not) could be logically characterized as a combination of such elements.[14]

The middle ground: ethnographic generalization
Most anthropological research is at the extreme of neither particularism nor global generalization. It is not so much concerned with the intricacies of any single fieldwork encounter or with universal principles. Instead, the task is interpretation (making sense out of ethnographic data) and translation (rendering these data intelligible to those not part of the fieldwork). Some of the prominent approaches are the following.

Functionalism
As a mode of ethnographic analysis, the objective of functionalism is simply to show how a group functions – to depict the group as a working system. An example comes from the father of ethnographic functionalism, Bronislaw Malinowski. Malinowski portrays a pattern of exchange in the Trobriand Islands known as the Kula ring. Kula partners exchange bracelets for necklaces between islands stretching for hundreds of miles, one set of items passing clockwise around the circle and the other counterclockwise. In Ma-

linowski's functionalist analysis, many aspects of Trobriand life – its myths, its belief in magical canoes, its mode of family organization – are associated with the Kula. The parts work together to form a social and cultural whole.[15]

Configurationalism

Configurationalism resembles functionalism in showing how parts form a whole, but the kind of integration envisioned is, to use a distinction noted earlier, more "logico-meaningful" than "causal-functional." The point is not so much to show how the system works, as in the economics of the Kula, as to display the premises behind the culture and the way the warp and woof of life coherently flow from those premises. Ruth Benedict in *Patterns of Culture* depicted the premises of Plains Indian culture as "Dionysian," those of the Pueblo Indian as "Apollonian." The Plains warriors were ruled by an ethos of dynamism and bravado, of excess and extremes, whereas the Pueblo farmers had crafted a balanced life of moderation and harmony. Benedict, who was a poet as well as an anthropologist, was able to weave many aspects of each culture into compelling portraits organized around these premises.[16]

Functionalism and configurationalism are not so much separate schools of thought as different emphases that guide ethnographic description. Social anthropology in Britain traditionally has emphasized a functionalist sort of description in masterful monographs that show the workings of kinship systems, of witchcraft and sorcery, ritual and myth, kingship and chieftainship. Cultural anthropology in America has emphasized somewhat more the configurationalist approach. This is apparent, for example, in "national character" studies where the entire culture, of Japan, Thailand, Russia, Germany, or the United States, for example, is summarized as an expression of some overriding themes.[17]

Functionalism and configurationalism both illustrate holism applied ethnographically. A whole society or a whole culture is depicted as a unity, as a working system or a coherent pattern. As a means of describing a way of life, this kind of portrayal has virtues but also drawbacks. To emphasize the unity of the society or the culture is to ignore the diversity; to emphasize constancy is to ignore change. These characteristic emphases are necessary in order to simplify and summarize major features, but anthropologists have found it necessary to add other approaches better able to cope with diversity and change. One such approach is the case study method, growing out of functionalism, and the other, symbolic analysis, growing out of configurationalism.

Case study: a social drama

Whereas the functionalist and configurationalist portrayals emphasize the unified constancies of the whole, the case study depicts diversity, conflict, and individual choice. An example is Victor Turner's saga of a shaky-handed circumciser. Among the Ndembu, the African tribe among which Turner did his fieldwork, the tribal circumciser has aged so that his hand is shaky. Parents fear trusting their sons to his knife, and forces are mustered to oust him. Counterforces push to keep him in office. Matters reach a head one night when the old man takes the initiative by shouting for the circumcision ceremonies to begin. Drums are beaten, songs sung, and the people become engrossed in their traditions. Sensing a mood of reverence for the old, the circumciser shouts for the boys to be brought forward. Without objection, they are circumcized by him. Tradition and age win over the new, at least for a while.[18]

Here Ndembu cultural patterns and social functioning are portrayed not as a fixed model shared without question by all members of the group, but as what Turner terms a "social drama." Tradition is not given, it has to be won, through clever strategy by the old man. Cultural tradition is a force, but only one force in a social process. Such a case study shifts attention from the cultural and social whole to the experiences of particular actors, yet it does not violate holism, because the details are always grasped in the context of the whole.

Symbolic analysis

Symbolic analysis is a way of interpreting the meanings of a culture through detailed analysis of a particular form. An example is Clifford Geertz's interpretation of the Balinese cockfight. In Bali, cocks are greatly prized, and men identify strongly with them. Geertz analyzes cockfights as a symbol of the Balinese view of social reality. Balinese emphasis on status and hierarchy, on distinctions between high and low castes, is expressed in the fights; the ritual of the cockfight provides the Balinese a way of symbolizing and communicating cultural values.[19]

Symbolic analysis is to configurationalism as the case study is to functionalism. Like configurationalism, symbolic analysis endeavors to reveal the logicomeaningful patterning of a culture. Geertz's aim with respect to the Balinese is like Benedict's vis-à-vis the Plains and Pueblo Indians. Geertz gains precision, though, by focusing in detail on a specific form – a cockfight – and representing the whole through that part.

Ethnographic generalization

Whatever the approach, ethnography is always more than description. Ethnography is also a way of generalizing. This way differs from the standard scientific model, however, and in some ways is closer to the arts. The scientific model is based on principles some would trace to Aristotle. Inductively surveying many instances, positivist science ascertains a principle or trend common to all, or traces covariation. Commonality and covariation can then be stated as typologies, laws, or statistical correlations.

Ethnography generalizes too, but in a different way, in some respects more akin to literature than to science. Ethnography reveals the general through the particular, the abstract through the concrete. Just as Macbeth teaches about guilt, Hamlet about anxiety, and the parable of the prodigal son about love and justice, so do ethnographies teach general lessons. From the Kula ring we learn about order and integration; from the shaky-handed circumciser, about the interplay of tradition and conflict; and from the cockfight, about hierarchy. The Balinese cockfight and the Ndembu circumcision teach truths of human conduct, not in the way fruit flies teach about genetics (here experiments confirmed or refuted general laws) but in the manner of the play, poem, or parable.

Ethnography is unlike literature and like science in that it endeavors to describe real people systematically and accurately, but it resembles literature in that it weaves facts into a form that highlights patterns and principles. As in good literature, so in good ethnography the message comes not through explicit statement of generalities but as concrete portrayal. The readers must decode the description in order to grasp for themselves the underlying values, then juxtapose these implicitly abstracted patterns to illuminate their own experience, as well as that which they imagine to have been lived by the natives.

In light of this view of ethnography, one must regard with caution any method claiming strict scientific precision and objectivity. Formal methodologies, such as mathematical measurements, have their place in ethnographic description; properly employed, they can make it more precise. But from our standpoint, at least one aim of anthropology is literary – what Evans-Pritchard terms "translation"[20] and Clifford Geertz phrases as "thick description," which entails "the power of the scientific imagination to bring us into touch with the lives of strangers."[21] Ethnography can never describe with complete objectivity, producing a set of facts that are completely true; but through its portrayals and interpretations it can communicate human truths.

Deduction, experimentation, and introspection

Consider two remarks heard in rather different contexts.

In the vaudevillelike *ludruk* plays performed in the slums and shantytowns of Surabaya, Indonesia, one joke that incites the audience to roll in the aisles is this: A clown asks, "How many turns are between the cities of Surabaya and Banyuwangi?" When his companion cannot answer, the clown responds to his own question: "Two. Left and right!"

During a lecture held off Logic Lane at Oxford, a philosopher informed his students: "I am thinking; should I doubt that I am thinking, my doubting is itself thinking; hence my doubt confirms my proposition."

How are the Surabaya clown and the Oxford philosopher alike? Both win their point by a clever and tricky argument that is more deductive than inductive, though in different ways.

The clown's question appears to be empirical, one that could be answered by factual research: counting the turns between the two cities. His trick is to answer at a level more abstract than the question. He states not how many turns but how many kinds of turns. To give that answer, he need not carry out research; he need only think logically. He subdivides the category "turn" into its component parts, left and right. He gives a deductive answer to a seemingly inductive question.

The Oxford philosopher defines "thinking" to include doubt.

Given this premise (and only if one accepts it), the conclusion is assured. Again, the argument is won by reasoning out logical implications of a category – by a kind of deduction.

The clown and the philosopher, then, both reason deductively. What about the anthropologist? He differs from the two in that much of his research is empirical or inductive: based on gathering facts. He does not simply think, he looks and listens, photographs and records, then laboriously combs through his data and formulates his findings. At least, this is part of his work. Is it all of it? No, anthropological research is deductive too. More than is often realized, anthropological research depends on thinking, on the manipulation of logical categories. How else would anthropologists formulate the questions to be investigated, decide how to formulate and analyze their data, and compose their ethnographies? Nevertheless, the emphasis and style of anthropological research is concrete, inductive, empirical. The anthropologist is less like the clever clown than the clod who laboriously counts the turns between Surabaya and Banyuwangi, but he is not quite like that one either; as he plodded along, counting, the anthropologist would probably notice that turns not only went left and right but also swerved, climbed, and descended in subtle patterns so that he would formulate a theory of topography more subtle than that which divides all turns into left and right. Anthropology is based on an interplay between deduction and induction.

The philosopher's statement is based not only on deduction but also on introspection. He not only reasons logically, he also inquires about his own thoughts and feelings. In this example, he does not probe deeply in his inner life, but he does set the stage for introspection by indicating a conclusion he would draw if he perceived a certain emotion (doubt) in himself. The general point is this: A characteristic way that philosophy reasons is introspectively; the philosopher looks within and reasons about what he sees. The most famous example of this is the slogan coined by Descartes: "I think, therefore I am."

The German philosopher Lichtenberg wittily extended Descartes's slogan to others when he concluded, "They do not think, therefore they do not exist."[22] This slogan, too, exemplifies a characteristic way of philosophizing. The philosopher looks within, then looks without, generalizing about others on the basis of himself. In that kind of philosophy known as "phenomenology," for example, the philosopher probes his own experience deeply – his perceptions of time, his views of morality, and the like – then reasons from this about the categories of human experience in general. If this sounds silly – everybody is different, so how can you learn about human nature by examining yourself – remember that introspection claims a very solid justification: All that you can ever know is your own experience.

So much for the philosopher; what about the anthropologist? On the face of it, anthropology would seem to be as strongly other-oriented as philosophy is self-oriented. The crux of fieldwork is confronting the other, transporting oneself to a place as different from home as possible, there to learn about human nature in an utterly alien setting. When anthropology generalizes, it does so on the basis of knowing many societies and cultures, not just the anthropologist's own. Of all the humanities and social sciences, anthropology would seem the least introspective and the most extrospective.

Why this extrospective emphasis? The simple answer is that it is risky to generalize about humanity based on a single human, yourself. Likewise, it is risky to generalize about all cultures based on knowing only one, your own.

This answer, though valid to a point, is too simple. It draws too sharp a line between self and other, subjectivity and objectivity, introspection and extrospection. It assumes that the anthropologist is merely a robot or clerk who tabulates data instead of interpreting them: "One more culture heard from," he announces as he marks down a trait of the fiftieth or hundredth case. It ignores the interpretive aspect of research. Because the anthropologist is a thinking being, himself *Homo sapiens*, he interprets; and interpretation entails introspection, albeit implicit. When the anthropologist does fieldwork, when he classifies and analyzes world cultures, he works not only with data but also with himself. No matter how objectively he attempts to record and analyze, he does so in terms of his own categories, attitudes, and orientations.

Anthropologists have tried to control for personal bias in two ways. One way is to systematize the research process so that the categories of the system rather than those of the self are predominant; this is done by using questionnaires, tests, charts for categorizing observations, and the like. Its disadvantage is that it rigidifies perception, so that one is less open to the subtleties of the other culture. The second means of control is to make personal bias explicit, to introspect openly so that the researcher himself becomes part of the subject of research; this is done through so-called first-person ethnographies, in which autobiographical insight is coupled with ethnographic reporting. The disadvantage of this is that attention gets diverted from the other to the self, sometimes excessively.

Objectivity is impossible, subjectivity undesirable, if one's end is understanding humanity in general rather than simply oneself. Is anthropology, then, folly? Perhaps, but not because of its inability to be either fully objective or fully subjective. In fact, the distinctive mix of objectivity and subjectivity, other-knowledge and self-knowledge, found in anthropology can be illuminating. Other-knowledge and self-knowledge enhance each other rather than merely compete. Consider this gradient: Insight into the self is best obtained through relation to another person (as in psychoanalysis, where the other, the analyst, helps the self, the analysand, "see himself as others see him," i.e., more plainly and objectively than is possible if one works alone); insight into one's own culture is best obtained through relation to another culture (as in anthropology, where representatives of the other culture, the natives, help representatives of our culture, the anthropologists, to see their own culture more plainly and objectively than if they stay at home). In fieldwork and even in comparative analysis, introspection and extrospection interact. Fieldwork and comparative analysis are not merely mechanical ways to gather data but are part of a reflection on self and culture that can alert one to what is unique and what is common about our culture. The trick is to grasp the other while seeing oneself (or one's culture) sharply in terms of the other. The danger is that one will see too much or too little of oneself in the other — excesses of subjectivity or objectivity.

Imagine watching a film. You empathize with the hero or heroine, identifying with that character as an extension of yourself. Yet while identifying, you also have superior knowledge; you see the total plot unfold, whereas each character is confined to its particular situation. You see, for example, the villains plotting to assassinate the hero, and you know what the hero does not: that when he steps around the corner, the villains will be there, waiting. You may want to intercede, and you feel pain as the character suffers, for that character is, in part, you. At the same time, you are the all-knowing observer who sees the whole as well as the part and views the action objectively. Imagine, further, that instead of a character crossing the screen, it is an entire culture, your own. Assume that while identifying with it, you also see its place in the wider scheme of things – its relationship to some other culture in which you are also involved and how your own culture is merely one instance of general principles. Here we remind ourselves of the kinds of combination of subjectivity and objectivity that are entailed in anthropological research, whether in the field or comparatively.

If encounter with the other is the distinctively anthropological method for obtaining a kind of objectification of the self, or of one's own culture, it should be realized that anthropology stops short of certain methods featured by other disciplines.

Psychologists, for example, gain objectivity by performing experiments. In them, the experimenter deliberately manipulates the subjects – which may be rats, pigeons, or human beings – in situations created by the experimenter. Fieldwork could be seen as an experiment: You dump a foreigner into a group and see what happens. But fieldwork is not so deliberately manipulative as the experiment, and the setting is "natural," that is, contrived by the natives rather than the ethnographer. The comparison helps us locate anthropology along a scale of objectivity. Anthropology is not simply life; it is not unexamined experience, that is, simple subjectivity. At the other extreme, it is not the laboratory experiment, where one manipulates subjects to inquire into certain laws or relationships – a method emphasizing detachment of experimenter from subject. The drawback of simply living is that it does not necessarily yield understanding, and the drawback of so objectifying a method as the experiment is that it loses the immediacy of human experience. Anthropology itself varies in its mix of subjectivity and objectivity, but most of its methods are located in the middle range of the scale.

The deductive, introspective, and even experimental aspects of anthropology are recognized more today than formerly. Some old-fashioned anthropologists may have seen themselves as going out simply to collect facts – going, as Thoreau once said, to count the cats in Zanzibar. Anthropology is, in fact, deductive as well as inductive (because it is guided by theory and other mental constructions of the researcher as well as based on facts researched), introspective as well as extrospective (because understanding of the other entails understanding of the self), and experimental (because one is actively participating in social life rather than passively recording data). Despite its containing all these elements – deduction, introspection, and experimentation – anthropology is distinct from such disciplines as philosophy and psychology, which emphasize them. Anthropology's distinctive emphasis remains understanding of human nature based on fieldwork.

Fieldwork, ethnography, and theory

We have treated three steps in anthropological research: fieldwork, ethnographic interpretation, and theoretical generalization. The anthropologist goes to the field to encounter the other, he describes and interprets what he learns from that encounter, and he generalizes about human existence on the basis of that encounter and other ethnographic data. The steps slide into each other and circle back onto each other, so that theory guides fieldwork just as fieldwork leads to theory.

As always, a crisp summary oversimplifies. Each step of anthropological research entails dilemmas common to any human inquiry: engagement versus detachment, subjectivity versus objectivity, particularization versus generalization, induction versus deduction, and so forth. Owing to the philosophical issues entailed at every step, a cookbook manual that lays out a fixed recipe for fieldwork is misleading. Misleading also is an overphilosophical discussion, which leaves an impression that the ethnographer is constantly in the position of Rodin's thinker, whereas, in fact, much of what he does in the field is routine: hanging his clothes out to dry after a tropical storm, recording household censuses, and sitting through endless social engagements. By tacking back and forth between the extremes of activities entailed, including what anthropology does not do as well as what it does, we have attempted to give some feel for the complexity of the enterprise as well as its direction.

At the center is fieldwork. As "participant observation," fieldwork is experience as well as method, but it is emphatically method and not just experience. The main instrument of this method is the fieldworker himself, but he must struggle to harness his subjectivity toward the purpose of the research, which is understanding of human experience that is somewhat systematic and objective – more so, at least, than casual impression or common sense. Nothing is less useful than an adventure without meaning, an encounter without notes, and much of the data of fieldwork come through rather tedious observation and recording. Yet the deepest insights may derive from a flash of understanding that comes from engagement and encounter. As the term "participant observation" suggests, fieldwork combines objectivity and subjectivity, routine and adventure, system and openness.

Fieldwork leads to ethnography. Though based on fieldwork, ethnography is also a way of generalizing about humanity. Like the novel, poem, and parable, but also like the scientific experiment, ethnography must say more than it tells; it must imply and teach general significances through presentation of particular experiences and patterns. Among the truths communicated are the ethnographer's as well as the native's, yet few care to read the confessional memoirs of an ethnographer. What is crucial is the truths of his interpretations, filtered through the experience and worldview of the interpreter, but focused sharply and precisely on the world of the native. A great ethnographic work is both scientific and literary, attaining a marked degree of objective precision, yet translating patterns discerned in the alien group into a form comprehensible to the reader at home.

Given the complexity of ethnography, it is obviously difficult to generalize globally based on ethnographies. It is wrong to synthesize merely substantive or "factual" findings of ethnographic investigations, for each ethnography is more than a report, a mere shortcut to being there. Each is an interpretation, a synthesis of questions, theories, and attitudes that guide the interpreter as well as facts reported. At the same time, the empirical or inductive approach characteristic of anthropological generalization is a necessary antidote to purely deductive or introspective efforts at reflecting on human nature. The danger in pure philosophy is that the truths discerned by self-examination may be too closely bound to the experience of the philosopher and the categories of his culture. Far from providing a smooth road to general truths, anthropology makes the journey appropriately rough.

We can now more fully perceive a meaning in the metaphor "soft focus." However glaring the light illuminating the object of ethnographic study, focus on that object cannot be precise in the sense of the lens narrowing its field to pinpoint only that object. In the ethnographic experience, the photographer is part of the camera, and both are part of the foreground being photographed as well as of the background that infuses the foreground. Accordingly, focus is necessarily soft or, in a deep sense, holistic, in order to capture the elements surrounding the object of focus as well as the object. The resulting picture is multidimensional, a kind of holograph that can be glimpsed with tantalizing clarity from certain angles, but that from others dissolves into hazy depths owing to the complex convergence of forces that create the image.

3

Significance

Your sons and your daughters shall prophesy.
Your old men shall dream dreams, and your young men
shall see visions.

Joel 2:28

Emphasis on culture and recognition of the subjective aspect of
interpretation link anthropology to the humanities, yet its striving
for systematization, generalization, and precise observation reflects
the inspiration of the sciences. Anthropology is an academic discipline, yet it insists on learning in the dust and confusion of life
as well as in library or laboratory. Anthropology is a product of
Western civilization, yet it seeks its understanding in exotic settings.

In short, anthropology does not have a simple, neat, unified vision. The dominant themes in anthropology are often opposed –
the scientific versus the humanistic, subjectivity versus objectivity,
particularism versus generalization, relevance versus the exotically
irrelevant. Furthermore, the discipline is divided into subdisciplines
and specialties that pursue their own directions, eroding any unity.
Not only are there archaeologists, physical anthropologists, sociocultural anthropologists, and linguists; there are a plethora of specialized researchers: One studies the economics of a remote tribe;
another, the knuckle-walking of the gorillas; still another, the com-
puterization of human thought. Many anthropologists would deny
that there is any overriding perspective. Yet forces in anthropology
press toward integration. Inspired by the tradition of holism, many
anthropologists seek some unifying vision. What has resulted from
this search? A number of schemes and theories have been proposed.
The most comprehensive of these is based on the theory of
evolution.

The greatest story ever told

The theory of evolution portrays the relationship of the natural to the cultural, the exotic to the familiar, ideational perspectives to materialistic perspectives. All these relationships are envisioned as a panoramic story. Humans evolve from "natural" beginnings to cultural endings – cell to animal, hominoid to hominid, and finally savage to civilized. Variation, whether biological or cultural, is explained by the principle of natural (or cultural) selection operating in varying circumstances such that each trait results from adaptation to a particular environment.

The earth is created. Inorganic forces collide, then combine to produce life. From elemental life evolve animals; from animals, mammals; and from mammals, primates. The natural habitat of the early primates – trees – selects for grasping hands and stereo-scopic vision, which equip the ancestors of humans to manipulate the environment to create culture. Coming down from the trees, these ancestors evolve a two-legged stance, freeing the hands to use tools. The use of tools in turn frees the mouth for functions other than grasping and tearing. One such function is speech. Speech and tool use require and encourage selection for large brains. Large brains require a wide pelvis for the birthing female, and a wide pelvis is also necessitated by erect posture, requiring a firm stance. And so the evolutionary argument goes, persuasively (and, of course, less glibly than as presented here) explicating functional interrelationships that evolved over millions of years to establish natural conditions for human culture.

The story extends from the hominoid ancestors of both apes and humans through the hominid ancestors of humans only. The hom-inids evolve from *Australopithecus* through *Homo erectus* to *Homo sapiens*. With the advent of *Homo sapiens* some 300,000 years ago, the body and brain of the contemporary human was essentially established, and humans began to evolve culturally. By some 10,000 years ago, some humans had moved from hunting and gathering to agriculture. Agriculture permitted concentrated population and permanent settlement. Settlement stimulated the development of cities. Cities stimulated the development of literacy and technology, which spurred further cultural evolution. Eventually came the in-dustrial revolution, modernity, and the atomic age.

This paradigm, which tells the human story in terms of biological and cultural evolution, has many advantages. Its greatest one is its scope. It provides a framework within which to fit the most diverse data and modes of research. Shrunken heads, potsherds, and exotic languages are removed from the status of mere curiosities and become evidence of human history and cultural pattern. Activities that some may regard as unsuitable for grown men and women are shown to have their uses: Expeditions in the jungle, digging in the desert, and living among primitives all contribute to understanding the evolutionary story. Old bones become missing links, and old stones become lost cities; such finds have significance in filling out the story of humankind.

Stories create suspense, and suspense resolves into discovery. If any part of anthropology has captured the popular imagination, it is the act of discovery. It is hardly news when anthropology advances theory or method, but to discover a *thing* is newsworthy. The popular media are keen to report a discovery – of a lost city or a yet older skull – for a discovery is tangible, an event. As illustrated in popular films depicting the archaeological expedition as a great adventure, the discovery can also be dramatic: the rugged hero, accompanied by a beautiful heroine, braves incredible dangers to find the thing, the jewel guarded by the monster, which is the key to some secret of life. Here the science of archaeology is incorporated into the myth of the quest, which has ancient roots in human civilization but continues to surface in modern fantasy. But even in scholarly images the event of discovery can be dramatic. In one documentary shown on television, an archaeologist wonders whether European cave dwellers might have been horsemen. The camera zooms in on an ancient sculpture of a horse head; do certain marks on it depict bridles? The scene shifts to a Paris museum, which shows a British archaeologist. He has searched everywhere for an answer to the question, now he is about to find an answer. The camera zooms close to reveal that he is rummaging in a drawer. He removes the drawer and examines it on his desk. He finds an object and displays it. It is the jaw of an ancient horse, and he shows that the teeth were worn down in such a way as to indicate that the horse was kept in captivity. Here, perhaps, is evidence that ancient Europeans domesticated horses. In this scene, interest is focused on the act of discovery itself, and our interest is piqued through suspense; discovery of a thing adds another fact to the story of humankind.

Stories of human origins and evolution abound in human history. Every culture has its myth of human creation, and the story of evolution is within this genre (as also are competing doctrines, such as Creationism). But evolutionism is not only a story, it is a theory couched scientifically so that it stimulates research. Botanists and geologists cooperate with physical anthropologists and archaeologists as they all swarm around the dig, joining in so-called interdisciplinary teamwork to construct holistic syntheses of a past uncovered. Ethnographers are also useful, at least marginally, in that their descriptions can, by so-called ethnographic analogy, give clues about the living that help reconstruct the lives of the dead.

Moving beyond description, these scholars generalize in ways suggested by positivistic natural science. They shuttle between data and hypotheses in order to formulate laws that state general and functional relationships among geological, ecological, biological, and cultural variables. Such generalizations may be global, as in Service's law of evolutionary potential, mentioned in Chapter 2, but they may also be more restricted and precise. One archaeologist, R. MacNeish, states a set of conditions that are necessary and sufficient to permit the emergence of semipermanent hamlet communities with subsistence agriculture in the Tehuacan Valley in Mexico; such conditions include increasing population and sedentarism and increasing local exchange in markets. These kinds of generalizations are based on careful tracing of sequences in history – what follows what – and are sometimes supplemented by the comparative method, which traces covariation among elements distributed globally.

Whether at the descriptive or general level and whether in the activity of research or in its results, the evolutionary approach achieves impressive holism. The varied fields within anthropology as well as fields outside anthropology are deployed in providing a view of humankind integrated in two dominant aspects: the biological and the cultural, the contemporary and the historical. The paradigm is both narrative and systematic; a tale is told and relationships are elucidated.

Here, then, is a paradigm with many advantages. It catches the imagination of the laity and the media, while organizing the activities of the professional. It has the unity and scope to give coherence to diverse projects in anthropology, providing a framework within which these have meaning and legitimacy. It integrates the subfields of anthropology while overcoming dualism and paradox. No wonder the evolutionary paradigm was dominant in the formative years of the discipline and continues to retain support.

   Despite its advantages, the evolutionary paradigm, like all others, is limited. It encourages certain kinds of knowledge while restricting other kinds. Before addressing this problem directly, it is useful to consider some analogies.

Books, museums, and worldviews

H. G. Wells, the British pioneer in science fiction, expressed in some of his stories a vision of human evolution. In one story, a man travels by means of a time machine into an England many centuries in the future.[1] There he discovers a society divided into two races. One lives below the ground, working in the mines. This race has become short, powerful, and brutish. The other race lives above ground and does not work at all but instead spends its life in refining the arts. This race has become physically weak and psychologically effete. Wells's story combines evolutionism with a kind of social ideology. He dramatizes how, over a long period, the division between the elite and the proletariat could become exaggerated through evolutionary process.

   Wells's genre of writing portrays large-scale trends over long periods of time – macro processes of evolution. It contrasts to another major genre of fiction, which treats the intricacies of social relationships. In British fiction, such writings range from Jane Austen to the comic novels of Evelyn Waugh, P. G. Wodehouse, and Kingsley Amis. These novels are micro- rather than macrosociological, for they treat not large trends over long periods but the intricacies of manners and social relationships in some particular setting. (Think of Emma the arranger, Jeeves the butler, Lucky Jim and his peculiar academic colleagues.) The contrast is, in part, one of scale.

   Consider a similar contrast: coffee-table books and detective novels. Coffee-table books are large, colorfully illustrated, and expensive – suitable for display on a table. The subject matter is usually some vast process that can be presented through photographs. Some tell the history of the world's monuments, temples, and shrines, others depict the art or scenery of a civilization. The books capture the sights on a grand tour or the exhibits in a great museum.

The detective novels are not large, and are more likely on night tables than on coffee tables. Like the comic novels mentioned above, detective novels are microsociological. They treat the intricacies of social relationships as they swerve toward crime.

A third comparison concerns institutions rather than books, and it moves us back to anthropology. The example is taken from Oxford University, but similar contrasts are found in many academic settings. Consider the University Museum at Oxford. It has an important historical link with the theory of evolution. Here Thomas Huxley defended Charles Darwin in a debate with Bishop Samuel Wilberforce – a turning point in the acceptance of Darwin's theory of evolution in academic circles. In the University Museum, displays are arranged in an evolutionary format. Along one wall is the sequence from cell to primate to humans. Other displays elaborate this scheme, though not always explicitly; in characteristic museum-fashion, they display skeletons of various animals and even the skeleton of a local criminal who was executed. In this museum, too, is the Pitt-Rivers section, which contains cultural artifacts: musical instruments, weapons, tools, and some very large objects such as full-sized native ships and a huge totem pole collected by Sir Edward Tylor. These are arranged functionally, so that all things serving the same technological function are placed together, regardless of location or meaning in a particular culture. The University Museum and the Pitt-Rivers Museum reflect a macro perspective. Their exhibits are not designed to display the distinctive particularities of each human community or culture and the meanings of that culture for their members. Rather, they are designed to emphasize broad-scale evolutionary trends or technological categories.

At Oxford, anthropology is taught in several settings. One, the Department of Prehistory and Ethnology at the University Museum and Pitt-Rivers Museum, teaches a brand of anthropology reflected in the museums: a macro view, emphasizing material factors. Another, the Institute of Social Anthropology, teaches social anthropology. This institute has no museum; its layout is different. The

Institute of Social Anthropology has a common room on the ground floor – a rather shabby but pleasant setting for coffee and conversation, overseen by photographs of notable social anthropologists displayed on a wall. Upstairs, a library contains a range of works in social anthropology, that is, ethnographic analyses of particular groups and theories that relate to such analyses. An annex contains a lecture room. Lectures are held daily, and the week climaxes in a Friday-afternoon colloquium, which always stops promptly at six o'clock so that participants can repair to a nearby pub for further talk.

Resemblances are apparent among the coffee-table books, the science fiction of H. G. Wells, and the museums. Resemblances are also apparent among the novels of manners, the detective stories, and the Institute of Social Anthropology. The first group sees life as materialistic, as monuments and temples in photographs or as artifacts and specimens on exhibit. This view is informed by an evolutionary or similar schema that takes a panoramic, or macro, view. The second group is more concerned with a microcosm: the meaning of life to individual actors in their cultural context and the subtleties of social relationships. The Institute of Social Anthropology boasts few artifacts. It is a world of interpretation, embodied in the ethnographies on its shelves and the conversations and colloquia that interpret ethnographic observations. The result is microcosmic social analyses, which in certain respects resemble the novels of manners and the detective stories, though with the usual distinctions between literature and scholarship.

The evolutionary and the interpretive perspectives
The contrasts just illustrated are analogous to contrasts between the evolutionary and the interpretive perspectives.

The evolutionary perspective tends to an "objective" positivist stance. This is partly due to the large scale of the evolutionary perspective, so that life is viewed from afar in order to see the whole panorama. Accordingly, life is viewed, not engaged. All things and all creatures, whether fish or men, spears or boats, monuments or shrines, are treated as specimens arranged in display cases according to comprehensive schemes of classification, as in the University and Pitt-Rivers museums. If humans are seen as aspects of a process, they are seen as worked over by such massive mechanisms as natural selection, the process through which survival of traits is determined by the environment. The subjective viewpoints of creatures are of little interest and, in fact, raise the spectre of what evolutionists term the "teleological fallacy" (the fallacy that subjective purposes affect the evolutionary process, which, instead, should be seen as governed by the law of natural selection regardless of any petty motives and purposes of the creatures involved, including humans). Given the irrelevance of the actor's viewpoint, humans are treated as part of nature and analyzed according to natural laws. The metaphors and models guiding this view come from the laboratories of natural science and expeditions of natural history, not from engagement in social life.

Culture is the central perspective of the interpretive perspective. Culture is shared meaning. To comprehend meaning, one must see the world as others see it, to comprehend experience in terms of the others' frame of reference. This is the endeavor of interpretive ethnography.

Interpretive ethnography has no story to tell, at least none that is particularly striking from the evolutionary viewpoint. From the standpoint of constructing an evolutionary synthesis of human life, the hard-won insights and data of ethnography are often trivial. Bits and pieces of ethnography considered relevant by the evolutionist are not necessarily those significant for the ethnographer, and little of the classic ethnographic writing has found its way into evolutionary formulation.

Why is this? Ethnographic fact is relatively meaningless and trivial as object. It becomes significant as an account of the interplay between subject and object, the ethnographer and the "other" whom he wishes to understand. Ethnography is an interpretive endeavor, and the most treasured ethnographic interpretations provide not only substantive information but perspectives on that information. It is not the particular factual "findings" of a gifted ethnographer, abstracted from their forms of presentation and summarized as a set of facts or substantive hypotheses and generalizations, that are significant. Such abstraction would be analogous to listing as census or historical data a novelist's description of a place or characters. Certainly much can be learned from Faulkner about Mississippi, from Austen about early-nineteenth-century England, from Tolstoy about Russia, but facts are not the main contribution of literature; nor are they the sole contribution of ethnography. What is significant is the vision of someone's (the native's) existence interpreted through the sensibilities of someone else (the ethnographer) in order to inform and enrich the understanding of a third party (the reader or listener). Ethnography in this sense is like literature: as source of psychological and philosophical insight (and possibly of aesthetic pleasure) when read as an author's struggle to elucidate a perspective on life through his portrayal of a way of living – as he experienced it and analyzed it.

Here lies the problem. If ethnographic understanding is a product of the lives of the natives and the interpretations of the ethnographer (plus the responses of the reader), then such understanding cannot be summarized simply as "X tribe does Y and Z." Human lives are not specimens, to be captured, preserved, and ordered within museum cabinets or systematic schemata. Interpretation is powerful because it captures the interplay between subject and object, ethnographer and other; yet the need to capture that interplay rather than simply describe the object renders difficult the inclusion of ethnographic experience as part of an objective synthesis.

In sum, the distinction between the evolutionary and interpretive approaches is not so much substantive as methodological. It is not just that evolutionary theory concentrates on biology and environment, whereas ethnography focuses on society and culture; evolutionary theory can treat, as we see, society and culture. It is that the one postulates a different subject-object relation than the other. Accordingly, textbooks and other syntheses that attempt simply to "cover all the fields of anthropology" or to "present data on both biological and cultural aspects" fail to achieve true synthesis.

In fact, no final synthesis is possible, because the understanding conveyed in each ethnographic analysis shifts according to the context in terms of which that understanding is conveyed, and this context includes the reader and his setting as well as the natives, the ethnographer, and their setting. This argument does not lead to abandonment of hope for synthesis and a despairing return to the particularities of each ethnographic analysis viewed in its own terms; nor does it suggest that ethnography become autobiography or even fictional literature that is valued not for facts but for evocation of vicarious experience. The argument does suggest that at every step of substantive synthesis, awareness is needed of the relation between that substance and the method of which it is part. Even the evolutionary vision must be seen in context, not only as a provisional synthesis of facts about human existence but also as a worldview, itself a product of a certain epoch and approach. In short, one may endeavor not only to include ethnographic interpretation within an evolutionary synthesis but also evolutionism within ethnography. (A kind of ethnography of evolutionism was begun here and in Chapter 1.)

To sum up: The anthropological perspective is holistic, and it strives toward an integrative paradigm. But within it two major divergent tendencies are apparent. One reflects the influence of positivistic sciences; it attempts to achieve systematic and objective factual knowledge and generalization about humankind. This approach is illustrated by the evolutionary synthesis. The other reflects influences of the humanities; it attempts to characterize truths about humanity through descriptions and analyses that balance subjectivity and objectivity. This approach is illustrated by the interpretive ethnography.

Having set forth so stark a contrast between scientific and humanistic tendencies in anthropology, a caution is necessary. Like most such contrasts, this one is too stark; the scientists are less scientific, the humanists less humanistic, than in this simplified summary. Evolutionism, for example, may aspire toward the kinds of laws that a positivistic natural science idealizes, but in practice evolutionism falls short of positivist ideals. For one thing, the experiment is rarely possible in evolutionary studies; for another, interpretive analysis comes into play in evolutionary studies, especially with respect to cultural evolution where human intentions loom importantly. On the other side, objectivity is by no means lacking in interpretive anthropology. Meaning and intentions are not imputed to actors by whimsy. They are carefully inferred from forms and actions that are themselves quite open to observation and recording. Acts and utterances, narrations and performances, art objects and texts, are visible, audible, recordable. These observations and recordings furnish a somewhat objective basis for interpretations, and the interpretations themselves are constrained by public scrutiny at two levels: by the natives, with whom the ethnographer is in communication, and by fellow scholars or scientists, who form a community upholding certain canons of scholarship and science. In short, the evolutionary approach and the interpretive approach both have objective and subjective aspects, but the evolutionary model has more single-mindedly emphasized the ideal of objectivity while the interpretive model has recognized the interplay of objectivity and subjectivity.

We turn for a moment from theory to practice, considering the significance anthropology may have in the so-called real world. Here the distinction between the interpretive and positivist paradigms continues to be pertinent.

Implications for practice: the mastery of our future and the future of our mastery

Soon, astronomer Fred Hoyle predicts, the Ice Age will return, reducing the civilization of northern Europe to scattered outposts of igloos.[2] If not that, then the population explosion, environmental destruction, and crime may destroy us, if the bomb does not. We may have no future, but if we we do have one, we are challenged to master it by harnessing science and technology to fight destructive forces themselves derived from science and technology.

Even a technological solution must consider the human factor. After all, humans created most of the threatening forces. A human could push the button that sets off nuclear war, and human politics pose obstacles to nuclear disarmament. Less dramatically, humans resist the technology of birth control, destroy the environment for short-term profit, and destroy each other. Human needs and aspirations, cultural as well as biological, must be addressed by whatever solutions we attempt.

If humanity is a factor, then the human sciences are relevant to our efforts at solving problems. Among these human sciences, though, anthropology may appear the least relevant, for it deals with the exotic and faraway, not the familiar and close at home, which is where our problems seem to lie. This viewpoint is myopic. In fact, much of the tension between the superpowers is focused in the Third World, where these powers compete for allies and periodically veer into localized wars that profoundly affect us as well as the Third World; think of Vietnam. Then there is the Fourth World, that population of almost a billion humans who are starving, lacking medical care, and deprived of the minimal conditions necessary for survival; are they not our concern? Western industrialized nations are increasingly assimilating migrants from the Third and even the Fourth World: Hispanics pour into North America; West Indians and East Indians come to England; and Turks, to Germany. All of these migrations bring new problems of human relations as well as economics. Anthropology is virtually alone among academic disciplines in having extensive, immediate experience, through field-work, with the Third and Fourth World cultures that constitute the majority of the world's population and increasingly impact on our lives.

What practical contribution has anthropology made, and what could it make? A brief sketch of the history of applied anthropology introduces this topic.

Some uses of anthropology: applied anthropology

From the late nineteenth century to the beginning of World War II, anthropologists were employed by colonial governments – French, British, Dutch, and others – to aid in administering colonies in Africa, Asia, and the Americas. Some administrators were trained anthropologically, and some anthropologists became colonial administrators, but after the turn of the century the more typical pattern was that an anthropologist who had done field research in a particular locale would be called upon as an adviser with respect to some particular problem or policy concerning that locale. Viewing a policy in holistic context can show consequences unanticipated by the policy makers, for example, that eliminating African beer brewing for the sake of temperance also eliminated an important source of protein, or that eliminating the custom of paying for a bride to end exploitation also disrupted exchange systems sustaining social order.[3] Occasionally, advisers served dramatic purposes. In 1896 Britain was entangled in costly wars with the Ashanti of Africa's west coast, and in 1921 the wars threatened to break out again. An anthropologist reportedly was able to resolve the misunderstanding. The Ashanti king possessed a golden stool that was believed to manifest the collective soul of the Ashanti people. The colonial officials had insisted that the king give up the stool as a sign he abdicated in favor of British rule. The officials saw the stool as simply a political symbol, but for the Ashanti it was more. When they were permitted to keep the stool the conflict abated.[4]

The colonial period ended with World War II. Some anthropologists were put to work for the allied war effort. British anthropologists served in the Foreign Office and the Admiralty, some having responsibilities in former colonial areas that had also been sites for fieldwork, such as the Near East and Burma. American anthropologists were in military intelligence and the Department of State. Anthropologists contributed cultural knowledge to psychological warfare, prepared handbooks on formerly remote areas that were now strategic in military campaigns, and were active in combat (as when the British used some anthropologists to recruit and organize guerrillas in places known to them through fieldwork, such as the Burma mountains).

In postwar times, anthropologists have worked for the Peace Corps, the Bureau of Indian Affairs, the United Nations Educational, Scientific and Cultural Organization (UNESCO), the U.N.'s Food and Agriculture Organization, and other agencies. Unlike the colonial offices, these agencies are not long-term administrators of native society but short-term bearers of technical assistance. The anthropologists help marry the assistance to the native context.

A few anthropologists took active administrative roles. One bought a plantation in Peru and spent five years running it as an experiment in applied anthropology. The experiment was so successful that, aside from social benefits, the crop increased sixfold. Reportedly, the Peruvian government converted some other plantations to the system.[5]

Anthropology is now being applied in many practical fields – government, law, industry, agriculture, education. An example is medicine, the focus of a subfield known as "medical anthropology." One premise of medical anthropology is that a major problem in medical care is that of putting to work in people's lives techniques and technology already advanced in medical science. For instance, an overcrowded society would benefit materially from birth control. The techniques for birth control – pills and so on – are available, but the culture resists owing to strong commitments to fertility and large families. A family planning program must consider both the cultural context and the technology, and anthropologists have worked toward programs that attempt to do this.

The general problem exemplified here is sometimes termed "health care delivery." Available medical techniques meet cultural resistance. A study of health care among varied ethnic groups in

Miami, for example, showed cultural as well as physical barriers to using clinics and hospitals.[6] An anthropological study of a feminist clinic in Massachusetts showed how the cultural patterning of the feminist movement affected health-care delivery.[7] An anthropological study of working-class women in Egypt showed how their distinctive cultural images of the body affected use of contraceptives.

Research on psychic-healing clinics in California, gynecology in Yugoslavia, family planning in Venezuela, native views of healing in Ecuador, the culture of cancer, doctor-patient relations in cross-cultural settings – these are a few examples of anthropological research that bears on medical practice. One physician who is also a medical anthropologist argues that medical anthropology should revolutionize medical practice, forcing it into a holistic concern with the sociocultural context of disease and health and out of a narrowly biological and psychological focus that is as remarkable for its limitations as for its scientific advances.[8] Such a direction accords with the holism of anthropology as well as some other approaches.

Recognizing the increasing efforts of individual anthropologists to apply their discipline practically, some of the professional anthropological organizations have supported the endeavor. The American Anthropological Association, for example, has established, in addition to long-standing units in physical anthropology, archaeology, linguistics, and sociocultural anthropology, a fifth unit, for applied anthropology.[9] The association has also established fellowships and a placement service to position anthropologists in contexts (such as congressional committees) where they can contribute.[10] At the same time, the association has established a code of ethics (entitled the Principles of Professional Responsibility) that sets forth guidelines for the social role of anthropology.[11]

Aside from monitoring and facilitating the activities of individual applied anthropologists, groups such as the American Anthropological Association address social issues pertinent to the entire profession. Archaeologists, for example, have been involved in creating laws that would block the stealing of a culture's treasures by criminals who sell to wealthy collectors – a lucrative and worldwide business. (This is entitled the Act to Implement the Convention on the Means of Prohibiting and Preventing the Illicit Import, Export, and Transfer of Ownership of Cultural Property.)[12] By resolutions and other statements addressing appropriate agencies, the association has also worked to block destruction of human treasures – tribal cultures being destroyed by encroachments of modernity.

These resolutions and statements of creed are all abstract – the actions of a bureaucratically organized professional association. They formulate and express, however, ethical principles that anthropologists are led to consider owing to their personal ethnographic engagements. Paternalism and taints of exploitative ideology of course remain (after all, this is an American association attempting to legislate morality and action through clumsy bureaucratic mechanisms), but the attitude does seem to have changed since the days of amateur archaeologists blithely smuggling treasures out of Greece or Egypt for European museums, and of James George Frazer, author of thirteen volumes on the customs of "savages," who, when asked if he had ever seen one, replied, "God forbid!"

Why anthropology is necessarily applied

If anthropology is a scholarly discipline, then its primary task is scholarship.

Granted this, the functions of applied anthropology array themselves in opposition to this primary task. One may summarize these functions as three: problem solving, administration, and outreach. Problem solving entails making plans and policy. Administration entails implementing such policies. Outreach entails spreading the word, publicizing what is being done and why. All of this is commonplace, true of any kind of effort at "doing good." Even academic disciplines do these things; they are applied, administered, and taught; otherwise academics really do live in the mythical ivory tower.

Anthropology is, however, distinctive, owing to its primary method of scholarship: fieldwork. In its scholarly research, anthropology is already applied because it is involved with human groups through participant observation. In fieldwork, the anthropologist faces ethical questions, he must solve practical tasks, and, like it or not, both he and the group are affected. My first fieldwork in Indonesia threw me into certain dealings to get money for an impoverished family with whom we were living. More than twenty years later, I still participate in the subsistence of another Indonesian family, whose breadwinner, my close friend, has disappeared because of political persecution. Recently, a child from the first family has, through remarkable coincidence, come to live near us and has become involved in our life somewhat as we once were in his family's. Fieldwork may have lofty academic purpose, but it is carried out in a context of human need and human relations, from which one does not escape.

At a more abstract level, fieldwork with a group must be construed by that group, for these are living people. In my second fieldwork, also in Indonesia, the fundamentalist Muslim movement among whom I worked did this quite directly. When I took part in their training camp, they described me, humorously, as their "research branch." I was asked to speak at meetings in order to share my perceptions of them with them. When I finally published a book about them, a portion of which has been translated into Indonesian, one of their leaders wrote a preface in which he astutely described how he saw my role (he emphasized how I was always taking notes, putting me in my place as an observer as well as participant).[13] In my current fieldwork, among certain fundamentalist groups in Appalachia, elders recognize that our tapes and videotapes preserve their history. These last two examples illustrate a common way that the anthropologist is viewed: in one of his more comfortable roles, wherein he documents the group's life so as to commemorate and illuminate that life for those who are living it, as well as their descendants.

None of these activities was planned as "applied anthropology." Like the commonplace fieldwork of most ethnographers, they grew out of relationships that were part of the research process.

Does such a method compromise the purity of scholarship? In a narrow sense, it can. For example, information may be concealed in order to protect an informant's or a group's reputation; here the relationship takes precedence over pure knowledge. In a broader sense, this question requires a reconsideration of what is meant by ethnographic knowledge. What the ethnographer learns is not only the objective "facts" that the informant may recite but also the *relationship* with the informant. One aspect of that relationship is the trust between ethnographer and informant, which may dictate that in certain circumstances the ethnographer does *not* tell all. This ethical stance follows from the interpretive perspective, noted in

Chapter 2, which reminds us that ethnography communicates the ethnographer's experience of a way of life; the trust is one aspect of that experience.

An example from fieldwork: I attend a training camp held by the Muhammadijah. There I hear a talk by one of the leaders of the movement. Several years later, I write a book about Muhammadijah that includes a synopsis of this talk. I state the real name of this speaker as well as other Muhammadijah leaders. I send the manuscript to Muhammadijah for their review (something I did voluntarily; they did not request this). The speaker has now been elected to a high office in the Indonesian government and, presumably to avoid political risk, he asks that his name be deleted. I do so. Here an ethical value (that the ethnographer should not place an informant needlessly at risk) results in the loss of a fact. At the same time, the act of omitting this fact is itself a fact. The first fact tells something about the object of study, the second about the relationship between the ethnographer and the object of the study.

Applied anthropology returns us to the understanding reached earlier, that cultural study must be understood to include method as well as substance; the portrayal of a "culture" should include within it not only the "what" of that culture but also "how" the ethnographer constructs that "what." This interrelationship between content and method is true of any study, but the relationship between the two is especially close for the ethnographer. He is part of the lives that are the subject of his scholarship. No matter how academic the topic pursued, if it is pursued in company with "natives" who join the ethnographer in interpretation of their way of life, his study is part of their life. In this sense, anthropology is necessarily "applied."

Positivist and interpretive models: implications for practice
Despite their differences, the positivist and interpretive models have much in common. Both work empirically – observing events in the world – rather than solely through introspection. Both systematize and generalize rather than confine themselves to literary or poetic evocation. Both entail subjectivity as well as objectivity because, after all, it is the analyst who does analysis; there exists no body of data independent of the analyst. Finally, both can be meticulous and precise. It would be grossly wrong to leave an impression of

the positivist science as analytical and logical, the interpretive approach as impressionistic or intuitive. Excellent work in either vein requires meticulous analysis.

An important difference concerns procedure. In the positivist model, systematic observation or experiment leads to tests of hypotheses and formulation of general laws. Laws, in turn, subsume and thus explain specific phenomena such as the results of the observations and experiments. This kind of model is known as "hypothetico-deductive"; an experiment tests a hypothesis that is deducted from a law or theory.

Science, so conceived, leads to engineering. Experiments lead to laws, and the laws lead to applications. Laws of electricity developed through physics are worked through by the electrical engineer to the point of drawing blueprints that indicate the placement of conduit and wire to compose electrical circuits that illuminate buildings and run machines.

Emulating this positivist model of science and engineering, applied anthropology would be social engineering. Just as the engineer bases his blueprints on physics, so the anthropologist would follow principles of social and cultural anthropology in designing his blueprints for social and cultural change.

Even this scientific model harbors uncertainty at the point when knowledge is applied. This uncertainty lies in two areas. The first concerns knowledge. Even in science, correlations are not absolute, they are only probable. One can be certain only to a degree (which one can estimate through mathematics) that, if x happens, y will also happen. One reason for this is that in the world there are always complicating factors; x happens, but also z. Although vexing in the natural sciences, this uncertainty is all the greater in the social sciences because of the complexities of human conduct and thought.

The second area of uncertainty concerns values. Even if you have perfect knowledge, you still have to decide what to do. Assume that you have a scientific theory that perfectly informs you how to industrialize the Third World. Will you do it? The answer depends on your values. Perhaps you value agrarian and traditional ways of life more than industrial and modern ways of life; so you hesitate. (Such dilemmas drove President Harry Truman to request an "economist with one hand"; his economic advisers, Truman complained, were always saying, "But on the other hand...")

The interpretive model includes all of the foregoing considerations but also goes beyond them. It would not admit that perfectly objective knowledge of a situation is possible; knowledge is always relative to the knower. The positivist model can, in fact, be included within the interpretive perspective by always considering not only the knowledge postulated but also the context of that postulating: What are the premises behind it? What kinds of biases does it reflect? Such considerations force the theory and its implications for practice to be couched provisionally, while prohibiting presentation of a plan of action as though it follows objectively and automatically from scientific law and fact.

Where does this leave the activist? Here we can profit from the analysis and the example of Max Weber, from whose thought much of the foregoing is drawn. Weber argued vigorously that the analyst must be absolutely clear about his limitations. To fail to be so, while couching the analysis in the aura of certainty that the laity impute to science, is to mislead, and to mislead in a matter of choice that leads to action with serious consequences for humanity can be more serious than to mislead in knowledge alone.[14]

Should the analyst, then, withdraw from action? This was not Weber's conclusion. He was himself active in politics; he was an administrator; he was an architect of Germany's reconstruction after World War I. He neither prescribed nor lived a life of pure contemplation, but he insisted on clarity in defining the role of the analyst in action.

Despite the provisional character of his analysis of a situation, the analyst can nevertheless contribute to action. He can deepen insight. He can sharpen perception of how a given action may have a certain consequence and what that consequence may imply for the wider situation. He can even suggest costs and benefits of one action as opposed to another. But his analysis is necessarily imperfect, hence his recommendations, his decisions, and his actions – if he does act – are a kind of Kierkegaardian leap of faith. As Weber says, the difference between science and faith is only a hair, and action requires that the scientist cross that line.

The relevance of irrelevance: anthropology as antidote
Pressing problems, from hunger and overpopulation to the ever-present threat of nuclear holocaust, worry us. At closer hand, we

are aware – though we try to block that awareness – of suffering and misery. We read of the seemingly hopeless overpopulation and starvation of the masses in India, Africa, or Java, but need only look around us to see the cold and hungry.

If proximate human tragedies do not move us, then who can ignore the systematic tragedies – the seemingly unstoppable destruction of the environment by everyone from developers to government, the accelerating nuclear arms race, the blatant excesses of a consumer-infatuated economy? Anthropologists mourn the decimation of tribal peoples as so-called civilization destroys their habitats.

Facing these situations, one cannot but feel moved, by guilt if nothing else, to "do something." Western values favor action, an emphasis not lost in anthropology, hence the thrusts toward application and engagement. Service, whether in medicine, social work, or the like is, even in our individualistic, egoistic society, the most unambiguously justifiable kind of work. Any endeavor that does not directly and obviously contribute to survival and alleviation of suffering necessarily is questioned, perhaps most of all by its practitioners.

Anthropology, like many other academic fields, is placed on the defensive by pragmatic considerations. Of course, it is true that anthropology is necessarily applied in that it does its research among people, and every fieldworker finds himself engaged in affecting the lives of the group among whom he works, for better or for worse. It is also true that some anthropology is being systematically applied. But the findings of anthropology are often esoteric and difficult to relate easily to practical problems. In natural science, the relationship between theory and application is clear; everyone realizes that antibiotics could not have been developed without biochemistry, nor could computers have been developed without mathematics. But in the liberal arts, including anthropology, the relationship of theory and application is not so obvious. Interpretive considerations render that relationship even more problematic.

The challenge of relevance is met by anthropology in two ways. The first is by applied anthropology. Despite all the complexities of harnessing anthropological knowledge to practice, an impressive corps of applied anthropologists forge ahead in practical fields. Applied anthropology may sometimes look like common sense, but careful examination often discloses an uncommon sense. The holism, the sensitivity to culture, the method of participation observation – in short, the anthropological perspective – have demonstrated their utility with surprising cogency in a variety of practical projects.

The ultimate justification for studying anthropology does not lie, however, in the solution of this or that practical problem. Nor should a discipline need to justify itself in such narrowly practical terms. An entirely pragmatic emphasis is not viable, even if one's criterion for usefulness is that an activity contribute to survival of the species. To take an analogy with biology, it is clear that the organism must not only adapt to immediate environmental pressures but must also solve other problems; it must, for example, reproduce. Otherwise, no matter how shrewd each practical solution, the species will die out. Reproduction entails complex genetic processes for preserving patterns of adaptation by transmitting them to the next generation. Social theorist Talcott Parsons put the matter more comprehensively when he argued that any system, whether biological, social, or personal, must perform at least two kinds of functions: on the one hand, "adaptive" – which entails generating and mobilizing resources to solve "practical" problems – and, on the other hand, "pattern-maintenance." This second function is analogous to reproduction in biology; it entails preserving and transmitting the patterns that guide all processes within the system, including the adaptive. In a society, the economic, political, and service institutions most obviously exemplify the adaptive function, while the familial, educational, and religious institutions that formulate and transmit knowledge, values, beliefs, and symbols – in a word, culture – exemplify the pattern-maintenance function. Should a system solve only immediate practical problems (i.e., only "adapt"), it would be crippled in its long-term adaptiveness, for it would fail to "maintain patterns," to preserve and transmit what is learned through experience; each new problem would be encountered in total ignorance, and each generation would reinvent the wheel. Furthermore, society would be like a riderless horse, lacking direction – a state some see us approaching.

In short, through a wordy argument for what may seem obvious but nevertheless is rarely thought through by those whose pragmatism is as simpleminded as it is dominant in our culture, one can justify not only pragmatic action but also the sustaining of a cultural grounding that is the basis of action.

Anthropology is relevant, then, not only when it distributes contraceptives or administers plantations. It takes its place among the efforts at reflecting on the deepest and most pressing issues of humankind. Such issues may be very general, such as: What is the direction of human history? or What is the nature of human nature? They can be broadly relevant, such as: How can we find community and meaning? They can be urgent, such as: How can we avoid nuclear war? The contribution of anthropology is to broaden the framework of discussion. Anthropology can inquire into the assumptions behind all perspectives, including cultural perspectives, and, bolstered by cross-cultural knowledge, can consider consequences in the broadest sense. Anthropology can consider, for example, whether current proposals concerning the arms race, the environment, or our search for community sufficiently consider the full spectrum of human possibilities or whether discussion is too narrowly constrained by premises of contemporary or Western culture. Whatever the issue, anthropology joins philosophy and other fields that push us to examine our conduct, our values, and our lives to consider the premises that guide us and the consequences of our actions, probing these matters as deeply, critically, and broadly as we can. But anthropologists are not prophets, and anthropology is not prophecy. Anthropology has its visions and dreams, but it can claim no divine source – only imperfect human knowledge. As should be abundantly clear, anthropology is rife with its own biases and assumptions. The anthropological perspective, like some others, includes the requirement that one reflect critically on it, even as one is guided by it.

Harsh light and soft focus

Harsh light etches forms sharply. In the clear air of the desert or mountain, the sun glares, exposing craggy peaks of mountains, straight lines of buildings, the sinews and wrinkles of humans.

In portrait photography, human faces are sometimes depicted through "soft focus." That is, the face is blurred rather than depicted with crystalline clarity. The object is not so sharply differentiated from background and foreground but instead melts into its surroundings as though seen in a mist.

Both of these seemingly opposing ways of perceiving inform the anthropological perspective. The anthropologist seeks his subjects in a harsh light. Traditionally, he has studied them in raw environments, undiluted by the domestication of civilization. And wherever he studies, he participates in the nitty-gritty – daily habits, from excretion to copulation, birth to death, as these are revealed in close contact rather than veiled through the myths and refinements of high culture. Seeking ancient and humble origins, among the primates, the anthropologist reveals again his taste for the elemental. In all these proclivities the anthropologist shares a worldview sometimes termed "realism" – a way of seeing favored by natural science and certain kinds of literature, art, and philosophy, as well as by what we call common sense.

Anthropology also favors a soft focus, in a certain sense. Lest they perceive too sharply any single object while missing its place in context, anthropologists peer broadly, trying to glimpse foreground and background all at once, even including themselves in the picture. Aware that any object, any act is a convergence of myriad forces, they endeavor to capture the whole field, necessarily sacrificing precision of focus for breadth of vision.

This dual image, harsh light and soft focus, distills some of the complementary themes in the anthropological perspective. Harsh light alludes to a no-nonsense realism grounded in detailed observation of life in raw circumstance, as well as a quest for the basic and elemental. Soft focus suggests an openness, a holistic breadth of vision that includes the world as well as the perceiver while embracing those shared understandings known as culture.

Yet this image, like the notion of "perspective" itself, only partially captures the meaning of anthropology. Any statement of the perspective of anthropology is merely an abstraction from the activities of anthropologists. Anthropology is what anthropologists do – what they discover, write, teach, practice – as well as what they see and think. The framework that shapes and the picture that forms from these activities will change as do the activities themselves, necessitating ever new formulations of the anthropological perspective. New uses demand new lenses; new lenses, new formulas to describe them.

Notes

Chapter 1: Substance

1. Edward Tylor, *Primitive Culture*. New York: Harper & Row, 1958 (original 1871), Vol. 1, p. 1.
2. Edward Hall, *The Silent Language*. New York: Doubleday, 1959.
3. Thomas Hobbes, *Leviathan*. Baltimore: Penguin, 1968 (original 1651).
4. Emile Durkheim, *The Rules of Sociological Method*. New York: Free Press, 1938 (original 1895), pp. xlvii–lviii, 1–13.
5. Emile Durkheim, *The Elementary Forms of the Religious Life*. New York: Crowell Collier & Macmillan, 1961 (original 1912).
6. Classic studies of such societies include Bronislaw Malinowski, *Argonauts of the Western Pacific*. London: Routledge, 1922; E. E. Evans-Pritchard, *The Nuer*. New York: Oxford University Press, 1940; Raymond Firth, *We, The Tikopia*. London: Allen & Unwin, 1936.
7. Walter B. Cannon, " 'Voodoo' Death," *American Anthropologist*, Vol. 44, 1942, pp. 169–81.
8. Victor W. Turner, *Drums of Affliction*. New York: Oxford University Press, 1968.
9. Gregory Bateson, *Steps to an Ecology of Mind*. New York: Ballantine, 1972.
10. Gregory Bateson, *Mind and Nature: A Necessary Unity*. New York: Dutton, 1979.
11. Bateson, *Steps to an Ecology of Mind*, pp. 458–9.
12. Evans-Pritchard, *The Nuer*, p. 18.
13. G. Clark, "Morbid Introspection: Views of Psychopathology in Victorian Britain." A lecture in the Seminar on the History of Medicine, Trinity College, Oxford University, Spring 1981.
14. Joseph Needham, "Chinese Alchemy." Lecture, Oxford University, Spring 1981.
15. James L. Peacock, *Muslim Puritans*. Berkeley: University of California Press, 1978.

116   Notes to pages 17–37

16. Max Weber, *The Protestant Ethic and the Spirit of Capitalism*. London: Allen & Unwin, 1976 (original 1920–21).
17. W. E. H. Stanner, "The Dreaming." In W. A. Lessa and E. Z. Vogt, eds., *Reader in Comparative Religion: An Anthropological Approach*. New York: Harper & Row, 1958.
18. Rodney Needham, *Belief, Language, and Experience*. Oxford, England: Blackwell, 1972.
19. Alfred North Whitehead, *Science and the Modern World*. New York: Macmillan, 1954 (original 1925), pp. 51–8.
20. Gregory Bateson, *Naven*. Stanford, Calif.: Stanford University Press, 1958 (original 1936), p. 262.
21. Ibid.
22. Lincoln Barnett, *The Universe and Dr. Einstein*. New York: Harper Bros., 1948, p. 8. I am indebted to John Baggett for his help in preparing this section and the next.
23. Ibid.
24. Ibid.
25. Ibid., p. 9.
26. Ibid.
27. Ibid.
28. Alfred M. Tozzer, "Biography and Biology." In Clyde Kluckhohn and Henry A. Murray, ed., *Personality in Nature, Society, and Culture*, 2nd ed. New York: Knopf, 1959, p. 233.
29. Neil Hickey, "Crystal Gayle: The Coal Miner's Daughter Is Tough," *TV Guide*, May 12–18, 1984, p. 35.
30. Margaret Mead, *Sex and Temperament in Three Primitive Societies*. New York: New American Library, 1962 (original 1950).
31. Franz Boas, "Changes in the Bodily Forms of Descendants of Immigrants." In *Race, Language, and Culture*. New York: Macmillan, 1940, pp. 60–75.
32. Edmund Leach, *Claude Lévi-Strauss*. New York: Penguin, 1970, pp. 16–20.
33. Claude Lévi-Strauss, *Structural Anthropology*, trans. Claire Jacobson and Brooke Grundfest Schoppf. New York: Basic, 1963, pp. 206–31.
34. For this observation, I am indebted to Thomas Hofer of the National Museum of Hungary.
35. Clifford Geertz, "Ritual and Social Change: A Javanese Example," *American Anthropologist*, Vol. 59, 1957, p. 35.
36. Ferdinand Tönnies, *Community and Society*, translated and introduced by Charles P. Loomis. East Lansing: Michigan State University Press, 1957 (original 1887).
37. Emile Durkheim, *The Division of Labor in Society*. New York: Macmillan, 1933 (original 1893).

38. Max Gluckman, ed., *Essays on the Ritual of Social Relations*. Manchester, England: Manchester University Press, 1963.
39. Mary Douglas, *Natural Symbols: Explorations in Cosmology*. New York: Random House, 1973; *Cultural Bias*. London: Royal Anthropological Institute, 1978.
40. Victor Turner, *The Ritual Process*. Hawthorne, N.Y.: Aldine, 1969.
41. Solomon, Asch, *Social Psychology*. Englewood Cliffs, N.J.: Prentice-Hall, 1952, pp. 451–9.
42. F. J. Roethlisberger and William J. Dickerson, "The Organization of the Primary Working Group." In *Management and the Worker*. Cambridge, Mass.: Harvard University Press, 1939, pp. 493–510.
43. Edward A. Shils and Morris Janowitz, "Primary Group Loyalty in Military Action." In Walter Goldschmidt, *Exploring the Ways of Mankind*. New York: Holt, Rinehart & Winston, 1966 (original c. 1960), pp. 296–301.
44. Turner, *Drums of Affliction*.
45. Geoffrey Gorer and John Rickman, *The People of Great Russia: A Psychological Study*. London: Cressett, 1949.
46. Gregory Bateson and Margaret Mead, *Balinese Character: A Photographic Analysis*. Special Publications 2. New York: New York Academy of Sciences, 1942.
47. John Whiting and Irving L. Child, *Child Training and Personality: A Cross-cultural Study*. New Haven, Conn.: Yale University Press, 1953.
48. Max Weber, *Economy and Society*, ed. Guenther Roth and Claus Wittich. New York: Bedminster, 1968 (original 1921–2), pp. 8–9, 20–21, 57. A deep study of culture would consider the symbolic forms that constitute meaning – language, ritual, the arts – and the subtle actions and interactions by which these meanings are created and shared. Studies of the semantics and structure of language have been particularly influential in shaping the anthropological view of culture. At risk of reifying culture, as though it were an entity existing independently of the forms, actions, and interactions that embody it, this chapter concentrates on the first step in cultural study: achieving a grasp of culture's general patterning and pervasive power.

Chapter 2: Method

1. Evans-Pritchard, *The Nuer*, pp. 12–13.
2. Boris Pasternak, *Dr. Zhivago*. New York: Pantheon, 1958, pp. 270–1.
3. Claude Lévi-Strauss, *Tristes Tropiques*, trans. John Russell. New York: Criterion, 1961, p. 17.
4. Review of David Maybury-Lewis, *The Savage and the Innocent*. In *The Times Literary Supplement*, May 27, 1965, p. 420.

5. Clifford Geertz, *The Interpretation of Cultures.* New York: Basic, 1973, pp. 412–17.
6. Alan Lomax, *Folk Song Style and Culture.* Washington, D.C.: American Association for the Advancement of Science, 1968; Roger D. Abrahams, *Deep Down in the Jungle,* 1st rev. ed. Hawthorne, N.Y.: Aldine, 1970; Henry Glassie, *Folk Housing in Middle Virginia.* Knoxville: University of Tennessee Press, 1975.
7. George Devereux, *Reality and Dream: Psychotherapy of a Plains Indian.* New York: International Universities Press, 1951.
8. Rodney Needham, *Against the Tranquility of Axioms.* Berkeley: University of California Press, 1983, p. 33.
9. Ibid., p. 62.
10. Rodney Needham, *Primordial Characters.* Charlottesville: University of Virginia Press, 1978; *Reconnaissances.* Toronto: University of Toronto Press, 1980.
11. Marshall Sahlins and Elman R. Service, eds., *Evolution and Culture.* Ann Arbor: University of Michigan Press, 1960, pp. 93–122.
12. Rodney Needham, *Remarks and Inventions: Skeptical Essays About Kinship.* New York: Harper & Row, 1974, p. 47.
13. Edmund Leach, "Rethinking Anthropology." In *Rethinking Anthropology.* Atlantic Highlands, N.J.: Humanities, 1971.
14. Lévi-Strauss, *Tristes Tropiques,* p. 160.
15. Bronislaw Malinowski, *Argonauts of the Western Pacific.* London: Routledge, 1922.
16. Ruth Benedict, *Patterns of Culture.* Boston: Houghton Mifflin, 1934.
17. Ruth Benedict, *The Chrysanthemum and the Sword.* Boston: Houghton Mifflin, 1946; Ruth Benedict, *Thai Culture and Behavior.* An unpublished wartime study dated September 1943. Ithaca, N.Y.: Southeast Asia Program, Department of Far Eastern Studies, Cornell University, 1952. Data paper No. 4.
18. Victor Turner, *Schism and Continuity in an African Society: A Study of Ndembu Village Life.* Manchester, England: Manchester University Press, 1957; Victor Turner, "Mukandu: The Rite of Circumcision." In *The Forest of Symbols.* Ithaca, N.Y.: Cornell University Press, 1967, pp. 151–277.
19. Clifford Geertz, "Deep Play: Notes on the Balinese Cockfight." In *The Interpretation of Cultures.* New York: Basic, 1973, pp. 412–53.
20. E. E. Evans-Pritchard, *Social Anthropology and Other Essays.* New York: Free Press, 1962, p. 61.
21. Geertz, *Interpretation of Cultures,* pp. 16, 26.
22. Needham, *Against the Tranquility of Axioms,* p. 33.

Chapter 3: Significance

1. H. G. Wells, "The Time Machine." In *The Complete Short Stories of H. G. Wells.* New York: St. Martin's, 1974.

2. Fred Hoyle, *Ice, the Ultimate Human Catastrophe*. New York: Continuum, 1981.
3. Clyde Kluckhohn, *Mirror for Man: The Relation of Anthropology to Modern Life*. New York: Whittlesey House, 1949, pp. 168–72.
4. Ibid., p. 171.
5. Alan Holmberg, "The Research and Development Approach to the Study of Change," *Human Organization*, Vol. 17, No. 1, Spring 1958, pp. 12–16.
6. Hazel H. Weidman, paper presented at the Medical Anthropology Roundtable, American Anthropological Association, Toronto, 1972. Also discussed in the *Newsletter* of the American Anthropological Association, Vol. 20, No. 10, December 1979, pp. 6–7, "Profile of an Anthropologist."
7. Sandra L. Morgen, *Ideology and Change in a Feminist Health Center: The Experience and Dynamics of Routinization*. Unpublished doctoral dissertation, Department of Anthropology, University of North Carolina at Chapel Hill, 1982.
8. Arthur Kleinman, *Patients and Healers in the Context of Culture*. Berkeley: University of California Press, 1980, pp. 384–7.
9. A.A.A. *Newsletter*, Vol. 26, No. 6, September 1980, p. 1.
10. Ibid., Vol. 17, No. 9, November 1976, pp. 1 and 16, and Vol. 19, No. 7, September 1978, pp. 1 and 11.
11. Adopted by the Council of the A.A.A., May 1971. In *Professional Ethics: Statements and Procedures of the A.A.A.;* Washington, D.C.: A.A.A., September 1973, pp. 1–2.
12. This act, H.R. 5643, passed the House of Representatives on October 17, 1977, and was brought before the Senate on October 19, 1977. See A.A.A. *Newsletter*, Vol. 19, No. 3, March 1978, pp. 1 and 22. "A.A.A. Testifies at Senate Finance Committee Hearings on Legislation to Implement UNESCO Convention on Protection of Cultural Property."
13. Djarnawi Hadi Kusuma. Preface to James L. Peacock, *Purifying the Faith: The Muhammadijah Movement in Indonesian Islam*. Menlo Park, Calif.: Benjamin/Cummings, 1978 (trans. Muhadjir Darwin, Pembaharu dan Pembaharuan Agama, Yogyakarta, Indonesia: P. T. Hanindita, 1983).
14. Max Weber, "Science as a Vocation" and "Politics as a Vocation." In *From Max Weber*, ed. Hans Gerth and C. Wright Mills. New York: Oxford University Press, 1946.

Index

Aborigines, 18, 25, 37
administrators, 63–4, 103
aesthetic form, 66
Africa, 44, 48, 82, 103, 111
All Quiet on the Western Front (Remarque), 44
American Anthropological Association, 105–6
Amis, Kingsley, 96
anthropology
  applied, 103–8, 111–12
  and code of ethics, 105
  defined, viii–ix, 7–11
  economic, 10
  linguistic, 6, 10
  medical, 61, 67, 104
  methods of, 10
  physical, 27
  social, 3, 9, 34, 37
  subject matter of, 8–10
  travel and, 51–4
anti-structure, 39
Appalachia, 61, 67, 107
archaeology, 8, 9, 10, 60, 94, 105, 106
Aristotle, 83
As I Lay Dying (Faulkner), 16
Astor, Nancy, 26
Augustine, Saint, 55
Austen, Jane, 96, 99
Australopithecus, 32, 93

Bali, 53–4, 82–3
Bateson, Gregory, 15–16, 20
"Bear, The" (Faulkner), 16
behavior modification, 16
"belief," definition of, 18
Benedict, Ruth, 81, 83
Berkeley, George, 22
Bildungsroman, 55

Blackberry Winter (Mead), viii
Bokelson, Jan, 4
Bororo, 16
British social anthropology, 7, 81, 97–8
Browning, Elizabeth Barrett, 3
Buddhism, 17
Bureau of Indian Affairs, 104
Burgess, Anthony, 61, 62
Burma, 104

Calvinist Puritans, 17
Capote, Truman, 61
Carnegie, Dale, 16
case-study method, 82
Castaneda, Carlos, 54
causal-functional organization of society, 35, 79–81
Christianity, 17, 18, 35, 55
  and Protestant ethic, 17–18
  and Protestant tradition, 12, 17
  and theology, 15
cities, 40, 93
classification, 28
collectivism, 13–14
communitas, 39
communities, small, 36–8
comparative method, 76–7, 87, 95
configurationalism, 81–2
Conrad, Joseph, 18, 62
covariation, 78–80, 83, 95
creation, Hebrew view of, 24
Creationism, 95
culture, 99
  academic, 30
  definition of, 2, 3, 4, 7–11
  and nature, 24–7, 29–34
  negotiation of, 74–5
  and personality, 44–5
  popular, 41